Revivals in Caernarfonshire

Iolo Griffiths

Published by Iolo Griffiths, 2022.

REVIVALS IN CAERNARFONSHIRE

First edition. June 26, 2022.

Copyright © 2022 Iolo Griffiths.

ISBN: 979-8201880989

Written by Iolo Griffiths.

Table of Contents

Introduction

Wales has often been referred to as a Land of Revivals, and from 1735 to 1905, many revivals have swept the country, with their beneficial effects on the morals of the people, and many people turning to the Lord from their wicked ways.

During this period, revivals came frequently enough for the last one to be still a fairly fresh memory, about 20 years back, when the next one came. Though many devout Christians long to see a new awakening, even the most recent one to touch Wales, 1905 is more than a century ago, and is known from history books, and not from the experience of living people.

While this book deals almost exclusively with just one county of Wales, Caernarfonshire, the situation there, with the initial immorality, and the succession of revivals, some local in their scope and others national, and even international, will serve as a microcosm of Wales as a whole.

It may be helpful to make it clear from the start what a revival is, and how it differs from an evangelistic campaign, to ensure that there is no confusion as to what is meant. The word "revival" itself is a clue, that it is primarily for the Church, as you can only "revive" something that has once been alive. The main result is that the Church becomes more fervent, and alive to God. The conversion of people from the World is a bonus that comes from the revival, and is not the revival itself.

In 1959 (the centenary of the 1859 revival) the Rev Martyn Lloyd-Jones preached a series of sermons on revivals, and highlighted some of these important differences between revivals and evangelistic campaigns.

A revival can be compared to a repetition of Pentecost, in the sense that the Holy Spirit comes down on a number of people together. As a result of this outpouring of the Spirit, the people present become aware of spiritual things in a way they weren't before, and are touched by the glory and holiness of God.

This may manifest as a deep and terrible sense of guilt as they realise their utter helplessness before God, under the effect of the Holy Spirit's conviction, or in a great joy at what God has done. It is not at all unusual for both phenomena to be witnessed in the same meeting, as different members of the congregation are affected differently. This will be noticeable in many of the revivals we shall be examining.

Revivals are always characterised by reverence, but this is not always true of evangelistic campaigns.

As people become aware of their sinfulness, and of God's love, they long to meet together to praise God. They also become concerned for the people who are outside, and feel they must tell them, which leads to a missionary zeal. The people outside then become curious by what's happening, and become converted.

Revivals touch a cross-section of society, affecting all classes, ages, temperaments and intellectual types, thus defying psychology's attempts to define a "religious" type, and also lasts for a while, and then passes. In some cases a definite date for the start and the end of the revival can be established. In the case of a psychological experience, the effects continue to be produced as long as the stimuli and factors remain present, but in the case of a revival, the effects cease, even if favourable conditions continue to exist.

The results of revivals are abiding, and by and large the converts remain steadfast, and come forward without being asked. In the case of evangelistic campaigns only 10% of the "converts" are expected to hold. As a result of a revival, a great zeal for God and holiness becomes evident in the people, which is not always as apparent in the case of an evangelistic campaign.

Illustration 1: John Elias was an effective preacher who killed off a fair in Rhuddlan which was notorious for its debauchery, and his preaching helped to trigger the 1832 revival

The effects of a revival might be dramatic. An example in the early19th century was when John Elias preached a sermon at a fair in Rhuddlan, which was noted for debauchery and sin, and killed this fair once and for all. During an evangelistic campaign, crime figures may go up, despite the appearance that religion is going up. In a revival, however, crime figures never go up, as even the unconverted are influenced by the moral atmosphere, as sobriety enters the life of the community, and the effects remain for some years afterwards. Revivals therefore create a revolution in the social and religious life of the area, and undeniably represents a moral force which uplifts the mass of the people.

Revivals do vary in some respects, as the onset may be sudden or gradual, may be unexpected or may come after a long time of prayer. It may break out in a prayer meeting, a preaching meeting, or even during an evangelistic campaign which subsequently becomes a revival. But a revival is always a work of God, and not of man, may start in a big city or a small hamlet. Man's work will always start in an important place like a big city.

God may use a great philosopher like Jonathan Edwards, a great orator like George Whitefield, or a great organiser like John Wesley to carry out His work, but at other times may also use obscure people like David Morgan, an ordinary minister of the Gospel with no remarkable gifts, taking hold of the weak things to confound the mighty. David Morgan was given a remarkable preaching gift during the two years of revival, but afterwards reverted to being a very ordinary preacher. Similarly, the Beddgelert Revival originated in the preaching of Rev Richard Williams, Brynengan, who was an orthodox, but not particularly popular preacher.

Phenomena may accompany a revival, such as conviction with agony of soul, groaning audibly. Sometime people are so convicted that they faint and fall to the ground, perhaps accompanied by convulsions or unconsciousness. The behaviour of people at revivals might include jumping, shouting and groaning, which would seem extravagant and ridiculous to outsiders, who are, understandably, suspicious of anything they don't understand or cannot explain. That would be the reason why revivals are often criticised, and why phenomena such as the "singing in the air" associated with the Beddgelert Revival, tend to be dismissed by sceptics as being the fruit of the hearer's imagination.

It might be difficult to imagine a link between pre-Reformation Catholicism and 18th and 19th century Nonconformity, but the Rev J Fisher, in an article in the Rhyl Journal of June 10, 1905, giving a brief history of revivals, describes the phenomenon of the "hwyl" as a mechanical trick, which became a feature of preaching in the 18th century, but which he thinks may be an echo of the Gregorian tines of pre-Reformation days, traces of which he claims may also be found in many of the older Welsh hymn tunes.

A vital difference from an evangelistic campaign, is that a revival is a miracle, a work of the Lord. Men can organise evangelistic campaigns, but only God can produce a revival. Charles Finney misled people by teaching that man can produce revivals by certain methods, but many people have followed these same methods, and failed to create a revival. If men could reliably achieve certain results by following a formula, and explain what had happened, then this would not really be a miracle, and thus would not be a genuine revival. Revivals don't need crowds, bands, choirs or any preliminaries. We can quench the Spirit and be a hindrance, but even if we follow all the rules we cannot guarantee a revival.

The real reason for a revival is for God's name to be vindicated, and for His glory. It is a demonstration of God's power, and does not need man's intellect and ability, and is not for man's glory. The risk of man sharing in the glory due to God could actually hinder, rather than help, a revival.

The futility of trying to create a revival by organised efforts is shown by the comment of H Elvet Lewis, an observer of the 1904-5 Welsh revival in his book *With Christ Among the Miners*. He wrote: "No amount, no form of organised effort could produce in 1906 what seemed as natural as a breath of air in the early months of 1905. I have seen, occasionally, an elaborate attempt to make it come; nothing was produced but disaster."

Origins of Nonconformity in Caernarfonshire

Although the great revivals of the 18th century and later owe much to the Methodist Revival, Caernarfonshire, unlike neighbouring Anglesey, did have a significant presence of the traditional Nonconformists in the form of the Independents, and to a lesser extent, the Quakers.

To understand the origins of the Nonconformists, who were to a large extent the heirs of the Puritans, we need to look at the impact of Puritanism on the county.

In 1650 the Parliamentarian Government established the Commission for the Propagation of the Gospel, with the task of expediting the triumph of Puritanism. The commissioners, with control of the revenues of the Welsh Church, were given wide powers, exercised through their "approvers", over the personnel of the parochial ministry, which they supplemented by a body of itinerant preachers.

The approvers were men of strong Puritan convictions, but Anglesey and Caernarfonshire could not boast a single commissioner between them. Nevertheless, the work of weeding out parsons who were considered unacceptable by the commissioners was well under way within a year of the passing of the Act. The real difficulty was in finding suitable candidates to replace them, and it took some years before even the skeleton of a Puritan parochial ministry had been formed in Caernarfonshire.

It was during Cromwell's Protectorate, which began in 1653 that the Propagation Commission began to bear fruit in Caernarfonshire, after the reorganisation of the Church under Triers.

About a dozen new incumbents satisfactory to the Triers were planted in various parishes in the county between Cromwell's seizure of power and the Restoration.

Of the dozen, three made a sufficient mark to merit mention. The first, Ellis Rowland, was from Anglesey, but it is unclear where he came under Puritan influence. It certainly could not be Beaumaris Grammar School, where he received his early education, and which had a strong Anglican ethos (with the Bishop of Bangor among its feoffees). Cambridge, which was rent with strife between Laudians and Puritans when he was there, is possible, but 10 years passed between his Cambridge years, and his appointment to a Denbighshire living in 1653, and nothing is known of this period. It was in 1657 that he was appointed to Clynnog, with Llanwnda added to it. The influence of his ministry may perhaps be seen in the fact that worshippers from Clynnog were among the persecuted Dissenters of Caernarfonshire 20 years later.

Henry Maurice was a Llŷn man, the second son of Morris ap Griffith of Methlan in Aberdaron. He was a nephew of Thomas Wynn of Boduan, and therefore a man of some social standing. He was only eight years old when the Civil War broke out, and when it was over, he went to Oxford when the Puritans were in power, and afterwards he was called by the Triers to take charge of the two adjacent livings of Llannor and Deneio, containing the borough of Pwllheli, and a short distance of his uncle's estate. He was there less than a couple of years. During that time he cooperated in the efforts of the great

Carmarthenshire Puritan Stephen Hughes towards providing a body of religious literature in a language that his fellow North Walians could understand. Although Dissent persisted in Pwllheli and 10 other nearby parishes after the Restoration, he cannot be credited with this, since he himself conformed at the Restoration, although he underwent reconversion some years later and became a leader of Welsh Puritanism.

Moreover, it is known that two years before his ministry began there were already "frequent meetings of godly persons" at Pwllheli, so he certainly did not initiate the presence of Nonconformists in the area.

It was natural that the men who were trying to fan the feeble flame of Puritanism in Caernarfonshire should seek to take Caernarfon itself, where the castle garrison would lend forceful backing to their efforts.

In the same year that Henry Maurice was sent to Llannor and Deneio, a John Williams was sent to replace the existing vicar of Llanbeblig, himself a nominee of the Propagation Commissioners. The name John Williams is too common to allow certainty in identification, but it is possible that he was another of the growing band of Llŷn Puritans, namely the John Williams of Ty'n y coed (or Castellmarch Uchaf) who went to Oxford to study medicine at the end of the war, and was one of the many Puritan suspects in Llŷn at the time of the Restoration, and a friend of Henry Maurice in later days.

The tradition that, although unordained, he preached in the Roundhead army, and even served as chaplain to Col John Jones cannot be substantiated, but is not improbable.

Whoever the incumbent may have been, it does not seem that the assault on Caernarfon had any immediate success. Until well into the 18th century, Dissent was a feeble growth there, subject to strong hostility from the townsfolk, and its few adherents largely dependent on Pwllheli.

The attempt to create a Puritan parochial ministry had failed even before it was reversed by the Restoration. Welsh-speaking candidates, who were also satisfactory to the Propagators or Cromwell's Triers, could not be found in sufficient numbers to go round. This posed the choice of leaving parishes vacant (as tended to happen in the earlier days), or grouping parishes under a single incumbent (a form of pluralism, a frequent resort), or to compromise by accepting candidates who, from a strict Puritan viewpoint, were sub-standard theologically, academically or morally.

In terms of the pluralism, it was no great matter for Henry Maurice to hold together the livings of Llannor and Deneio, since the two churches are only two and a half miles apart, and had traditionally been treated as an unit. But if, as seems likely, he also held Criccieth at the same time, which is another eight miles from the former two, this would make it difficult to maintain an efficient ministry.

Clynnog and Llanwnda, Ellis Rowland's parishes, were almost as far apart.

The fact that a certain amount of "dilution" was accepted under the Protectorate is shown by the fact that candidates which had been rejected by the Propagation approvers were sometimes accepted or reinstated by Cromwell's Triers. The readiness with which most of Caernarfonshire's incumbents conformed to the Prayer Book and episcopal rule at the Restoration certainly suggests that these incumbents were submitting outwardly, but had no true Puritan convictions.

A curious fact, and difficult to explain, is that Puritanism found its earliest footholds in Caernarfonshire in the very areas which just two generations previously were strongholds of Catholic recusancy. The separateness of Llŷn, and its closer ties with Ardudwy rather than with Arfon and Arllechwedd before the days of the road builders should be borne in mind.

An important link between Llŷn and Ardudwy during the interregnum was Morgan Llwyd, an Ardudwy man who, as an approver under the Propagation Act, travelled extensively in both Merioneth and Llŷn, where (as he recalls in one of his verses) he "lost his voice" through persistent preaching.

Although the little Puritan communities seem to be mostly drawn mostly from the lower ranks of society, they did have some adherents among the lower gentry, who also provided the background of the new Puritan ministry.

However, the adherence of some of these may not have been entirely sincere and disinterested. Griffith Jones of Castellmarch seems to have been aligned with the victorious faction for political rather than religious reasons. Thomas Madryn also seems to have been motivated by self-interest and love of power.

Jeffrey Parry, of Rhydolion, in the parish of Llanengan, on the other hand, seems to have been a more sincere Puritan. He held the rank of cornet in the Roundhead army, and, like so many of Cromwell's officers, used to preach to his men; detractors jeeringly described him as "a great Heaven-driver in Llŷn, and a zealous maintainer of Conventicles".

How he fell under Puritan influences, and what attracted him to the Roundhead army is unknown. Perhaps it might be through service to a Puritan magnate. His army career was no doubt in England, as it is in 1651 that he is first mentioned in Caernarfonshire, as one of the county "sequestrators" charged with the task of putting into execution Parliament's policy of meeting some of the costs of the war out of the estates of the vanquished. In typical Puritan fashion he named his son Love-God Parry, and the name (in the truncated and more non-committal form of Love) was perpetuated in his family down to the 19th century.

A few miles north of Rhydolion was Nanhoron Ucha, home of a small but well-connected squire called Edward ap Thomas ap Richard. The family was slower than some of its neighbours in adopting the English fashion of fixed surnames, but Edward's son Richard entered himself at Grays Inn, in the year of the king's execution, as Richard Edwards.

As a youth of 19 he no doubt absorbed some of the Puritan atmosphere of the Inns of Court. His marriage to a niece of Thomas Wynn of Boduan raised his stature in the county and provided yet another Puritan connection, since she was a cousin to Henry Maurice. Richard Edwards's importance in the story of Caernarfonshire Puritanism is mainly during the post-Restoration period, but he first comes into prominence in the county as a member of the assessment committee of 1657.

It is difficult to assess the impact of the itinerant ministry with any great confidence. The survival of small and persistent pockets of Dissent into the age of persecution is evidence that this did have an appreciable impact. However, the association of Puritanism with subversive politics and bullying militia captains would have created difficulties for the early Methodists a century later, who also had an itinerant ministry, although it has to said that the open-air preaching of the Puritan itinerant ministry may have aroused an appetite for spiritual excitement which was not satisfied again until the Methodists.

At the time of the Restoration many of the "intruded" incumbents who had been appointed during the interregnum were ejected, but since so many conformed to the Prayer Book, this was more of a legal than a theological matter, having to give way to candidates with a stronger legal title.

Ellis Rowland continued to minister at Clynnog for some months after a successor had been appointed, until in December 1660 he was locked out of his own church by some of his parishioners, while his supplanter officiated.

In 1661 Henry Maurice had to make way at Criccieth to the pre-Civil War incumbent, but he conformed and was given another living.

Despite being driven underground by persecution after the Restoration, Dissent continued to thrive. In 1672 the Dissenters came out into the open to take advantage of the Indulgence which allowed the licensing of houses for Dissenting worship. One of these houses was the home of Ellis Rowland, who after his ejection from Clynnog lived in Caernarfon, and in 1666 had been busy there distributing there a Welsh translation of one of Baxter's works.

Another of the houses licensed for Dissenting worship was Ty'n y coed, the home of John Williams (described here as "Congregational teacher"). He procured a second licence, for the same purpose, for Bodvel House.

No fewer than three houses in the parish of Llangybi were licensed, two belonging to the brothers Rowland (describing themselves as yeomen), who remained among the main Dissenters in the neighbourhood in the ensuing days of persecution, since the Indulgence was withdrawn under parliamentary pressure within a year.

It is likely that this upsurge of Dissent in the Llŷn and Eifionydd owed something to a resurgence of itinerant evangelism reminiscent of the Propagation period. In 1671, Henry Maurice, who had since 1660 been ministering in a number of English parishes as a respectable conformist, suddenly renounced his orders, and in the following year set out on a missionary tour of North Wales.

He was usually refused the use of the parish church, but preached sometimes in the churchyard, such as at Llanarmon, but more often in the houses of sympathisers, mainly at Pwllheli. He also stayed with Richard Edwards at Nanhoron, with John Williams at Ty'n y coed (who reproached him for his long neglect of preaching) and with some of his own relatives.

Maurice then left for South Wales, the scene of his main missionary activities for the rest of his life, but four years later he persuaded the distinguished South Wales Presbyterian James Owen to undertake a preaching tour in the North.

By now John Williams was dead, and the leadership of Caernarfonshire Dissent had passed from Llŷn to Eifionydd, more particularly Llangybi.

Pwllheli, as a busy market town, was too much in the public eye now that persecution had resumed, whereas Llangybi was a more desolate, and therefore less conspicuous, place.

Despite this, James Owen's congregation at Llangybi included two spies (as well as three genuine worshippers) from Clynnog, who informed the authorities, and brought the law down on their companions.

Subsequent encounters with the law, right up to the time of the Toleration Act, give evidence of the continued existence of a scattered body of Dissenters in South Caernarfonshire, drawing its adherents from a coastal strip from Criccieth to Llanengan, and as far north as Clynnog, ignoring parish boundaries, and meeting in any convenient central spot where shelter could be found.

A census taken in 1676 showed that there were just over 60 avowed Dissenters in the whole shire, seven of whom were from Caernarfon.

This was not much more than the number of Catholic recusants in the county, but there was one vital difference. The Catholics were a dwindling remnant who were spiritually starved through a lack of available priests. The Dissenters, by adopting the Lutheran principle of the Priesthood of All Believers, avoided this handicap.

The Quakers played a brief role in the county's religious history. In 1657 George Fox preached in Caernarfon, but had little impact. The next glimpse of Quakerism in Caernarfonshire is in 1672 when one Evan Jones of Llanengan published a Quaker tract (in English, surprisingly). A few years later we hear of a group of eight Quakers in the same parish, and in 1683 a few Quakers from Llŷn were among the emigrants to Pennsylvania.

Shortly afterwards, another Quaker meeting, in Aberdaron, was pounced on, and the dozen worshippers taken before the local magistrate. This group came from a range of adjacent parishes, stretching to Llanbedrog, and seem to have been mainly from the lower classes, except for one man of substance from Dolgellau who had joined them.

Unlike the Independents, the Quakers did not survive as a major force in Caernarfonshire's religious history, as the last glimpse of Caernarfonshire Quakerism is a meeting in Penmachno in 1731, addressed by a Pennsylvania Quaker (of Bala origin) who was trying to revive a waning cause.

The Glorious Revolution of 1688 which brought William and Mary to the throne also brought a substantial measure of legalised freedom of worship. Some of the houses which had been licensed for worship during the brief period of Charles II's Indulgence, and had since then been used occasionally, and clandestinely, when they could avoid the vigilance of the authorities, now gave more permanent shelter.

Richard Edwards remained a pillar of local Nonconformity till his death in 1704, and one of its meeting places (which he probably attended) was within a stone's throw of Nanhoron.

Ellis Rowland precariously held together the tiny remnant of Dissent in and around Caernarfon during the time of persecution, and in later, easier years he kept a private grammar school there. He was in comfortable circumstances when he died in 1693. In the last 15 years he and his wife had held the Llanfair Isgaer estate in trust for the infant heir.

From 1689 too the Dissenters of Pwllheli and neighbourhood had a regular minister in Daniel Phillips, a Carmarthenshire man and a pupil of Stephen Hughes. He had preached there occasionally since 1684, and had married the widow of Henry Maurice, and lived in her house at Pwllheli, which became a sort of manse for four successive ministers, until in 1741 (or possibly earlier) the congregation built its own chapel – the first in Caernarfonshire.

In accordance with the usual practice of the early Dissenters, Phillips exercised a general pastoral oversight over all the Dissenters of the shire, and the few who were to be found in Anglesey, and for this purpose he received small grants from central funds established by the Dissenting denominations from 1690. Worshippers in Llangybi and Llangian parishes, at Ty Helyg (later Capel Helyg) in the former, and Lon Dywyll in the latter, looked to Pwllheli as their mother church, going there for important occasions such as reception into the Church (the Independent equivalent of Confirmation), and receiving periodic visits from the minister.

The congregation at Caernarfon was in much the same situation. A handful of Independents had been meeting there since the Toleration Act. Twenty years later there were a dozen adherents, including yeomen, craftsmen and shopkeepers, and just one who styled himself a "gentleman". It remained a static group. Even in 1791, when the first chapel was built, it had to accommodate only 15 regular worshippers.

Origins of the Great Awakening

The revivals which touched Wales from the 1730s onwards and Caernarfonshire from the 1740s, were not an isolated phenomenon, but part of a move of God which is called the Great Awakening, which also affected Scotland, and in America was chronicled by the great theologian and revivalist Jonathan Edwards. In Wales and England this Awakening was marked by the origins of the Methodist movement.

Although these individual revivals do display some differences, they all shared certain features, such as a dissatisfaction with established religion, the importance of a personal experience of God, and an evangelistic zeal rather than a dry orthodoxy, and a need for society as a means of nurturing and maintaining the new life, and a deep awareness of the need for mission, and an expression of their faith and rejoicing through hymns of praise.

Most of the early major figures of the Great Awakening in Wales were from South Wales, so we need to trace the origins of Methodism there and in England before we can really look at how it affected Caernarfonshre.

The spiritual state of Wales was not very healthy. Many of the young people, although they claimed to belong to the Established Church, were in practice completely irreligious, and given to vain activities such as dancing, drinking and fighting. Erasmus Saunders painted a very gloomy picture of the spiritual situation in the Diocese of St David's (which probably would be an equally fair assessment of Wales as a whole), and it seems that the spiritual state of England was similarly discouraging as it said that Joseph Butler refused to be made Archbishop of Canterbury because he believed that it was too late to save the Church from the attacks of Deists (whose belief was basically that God created the world, but was subsequently indifferent to it, and did not intervene in the world through revelations and miracles) and Rationalists.

The fact that Joseph Butler's pessimistic prophecies were to be proved untrue was largely due the Great Awakening that started in the 1730s, which included the origins of the Methodists.

An important strand in the Great Awakening in Wales was the work of the Rev Griffith Jones (1684-1761), of Llanddowror, Carmarthenshire. He believed that it important for his parishioners to be able to read their Bibles, so that they could understand the Gospel and be saved. In order to do this, in 1730 he started his first circulating school. These schools were generally held for three months at a time, usually in the winter, when the labouring classes would have more leisure, and the aim was to teach the parishioners to read the scriptures in Welsh. This move was so successful that by 1748 it had reached every Welsh county except Flintshire. This movement, despite the insistence that all the schoolmasters had to be communicant members of the Established Church, was suspected by many of being a breeding ground of Methodism.

The Rev Griffith Jones was a great preacher, and firm in the scriptures, and his evangelistic preaching drew crowds, and was accompanied by scenes which could be considered a foretaste of the later revivals. He preached only in the Established Church, but would preach in numerous churches across Wales, and facilitated the printing of the Welsh Bible. He could be considered a morning star of the Awakening.

The Methodists were originally an evangelical faction within the Anglican Church, but faced suspicion, and even persecution from the Church establishment because of their affinity with the older Nonconformist groups, and in 1811 the Welsh Calvinistic Methodists finally became a denomination in its own right.

The very origin of the Methodist movement was in November 1729 in Oxford (and was then called the Holy Club), when a Mr Morgan, John Wesley and a few other serious young men who were studying at Oxford, arranged to meet together to read the Greek Testament. After a time they decided to start visiting the prisoners in the castle once a week. When they found that their ministry was proving beneficial to the prisoners, they decided to start reading and praying with the poor of the city, and donating money to enable them to buy food and medicine.

The year 1735 was to be a significant one in both England and Wales as three of the men who were to play an important role in Wales's spiritual development were converted, and the following three years saw the conversion of other men who were also to prove influential.

The great Methodist preacher, Daniel Rowland (1713-90) was converted at Llanddewi Brefi in Cardiganshire in 1735, after hearing the greatest preacher of the previous generation, Griffith Jones, preaching. Daniel Rowland was a deacon in the Established Church, and on the last Sunday of August 1735 he was ordained as a curate, and his labours at Llangeitho was the means of conversion of many before he himself was born again. At the beginning of his ministry, due to the lack of response from his parishioners, he adopted the evangelistic style of Philip Pugh, the Nonconformist minister of Llwynpiod.

Shortly after being converted the influence of his powerful ministry expanded, and in 1736 he started to preach outside his parish. He was possibly the first minister of the Established Church to help Howel Harris, and the first minister of the Established Church to be called a Methodist.

A few weeks after Daniel Rowland's conversion, Howel Harris (1714-73) of Trefecca, was converted on Palm Sunday in 1735 while taking communion in Talgarth parish church. The preacher, the Rev Pryce Davies, in his sermon, challenged any excuses his parishioners may have had about not taking communion, by saying "If you are not fit to come to the Lord's Table, you are not fit to come to church, you are not fit to live or to die." Howel Harris was convicted by this, and on Easter morning, resolved to be more serious, and attended the church on Whit Sunday, "labouring and heavy laden under guilt and power of my sin". An end came to his struggle when he was convinced by the Holy Ghost that Christ had died for him, and on June 18, 1735 he received assurance of salvation.

Howel Harris had intended to become a minister, and went to Oxford for this purpose, but he soon tired of the immorality he found there, so he returned to Wales and his friends. He started to counsel the sinners in his native parish and nearby parishes. He started to gain a reputation, such that crowds gathered to listen to him, and it is said that his words had such authority.

In 1737 Daniel Rowland was preaching at Defynnog, Breconshire, and met Howel Harris, and in the December of that year Howel Harris was at Llangeitho, with over 1,500 people listening to Daniel Rowland. This was to be the start of a partnership in an amazing outpouring of the Spirit. But they would also work with another man who had been converted at the same time across the border in England.

By 1737 Howel Harris had gathered his first "society" of new converts, at Wernos farm in the parish of Llandefalle, just north of Brecon. By 1739 there were 30 such societies, mostly in the south-eastern part of Wales. These "societies" are known in Welsh under the name "seiat", and were fellowship meetings, which ensured the nurture of the converts and fostering of spiritual life, by means of Bible reading, hymn singing, prayer, preaching, and discussing spiritual experiences.

Probably just a few days or weeks after Harris was converted, George Whitefield (1714-1770) was also born again, sometime around Easter 1735 after reading "The Life of God in the Soul of Man" by the Scotsman Henry Scougal (1650-1678), and after surviving a lengthy period of fasting during which he seriously sought God. In 1735 at the age of 18 he had joined the Holy Club in Oxford, which by then had 14 members. Their organised, methodical way of life had earned them the nickname of "Methodists". It would be in 1738 that he would meet Harris in Bristol, and that they would start a collaboration which helped to fan the flames of revival in Wales.

A couple of years after Whitefield was born again, William Williams, Pantycelyn (1717-1791), the great Methodist hymn-writer, was converted while listening to Howel Harris preach in Talgarth churchyard, in the shadow of the Black Mountains near Brecon in 1737.

William Williams was a student at Llwyn-llwyd school, who was aiming at a career as a doctor. In 1740 he was ordained as a deacon, but because of his involvement with the Methodists his application for ordination to the priesthood was rejected, and he joined the Methodists.

Another early convert of Howel Harris's ministry was Howel Davies who had come to Talgarth in 1737 as a schoolmaster. In 1739 he was ordained as a deacon, and the following year as a curate, serving under the Rev Griffith Jones at Llandeilo Abercywyn, in Carmarthenshire, until 1741, when he moved to Pembrokeshire.

In 1738 both the Wesley brothers were converted. Charles (1707-1778) was born again on May 21, and his brother John (1703-1791) likewise became a child of God just three days later after reading Luther's preface to the book of Galatians.

This wave of important conversions was part of something momentous happening in England and Wales, under God's initiative, and heralded the start of what came to be known as the First Great

Awakening, or more prosaically as The Methodist Revival, which continued throughout the rest of the 18th century, in a series of waves of Revival in Wales. Although this Revival was associated with the rise of Methodism, it also had the beneficial side-effect of quickening the older Nonconformist movements, which at that time were somewhat moribund.

Interestingly, among the three Englishmen converted in that period of three years, there was a great apostle (John Wesley), a great preacher (George Whitefield) and a great worship leader (Charles Wesley). The Welsh converts showed a similar division of giftings, with Howel Harris's gift being primarily apostolic, Daniel Rowland was the preacher, and William Williams, Pantycelyn the worship leader.

What is even more astounding is how quickly which these men emerged into a full-blown, Spirit-filled ministry. The fact that they had been engaged in preaching to some extent, even before they were converted, may be a possible explanation, though it may also be a reflection on the desperate need of the time that they did not serve a lengthy apprenticeship. It was just two years after Harris's conversion that preaching led to the conversion of William Williams, the man who was to become the greatest hymn-writer that Wales has ever known.

George Whitefield first visited Wales in the spring of 1739. He met up with Howel Harris on this visit, and they travelled together for part of the time. It was the beginning of what would become a very important partnership, during which Whitefield would have something of an apostolic role in the early days of the Methodist movement in Wales. Whitefield's apostolic role became less important as time went on, and the Welsh leaders, Daniel Rowland and Howel Harris developed their own spheres of influence.

John Wesley's first visit to Wales was several months after Whitefield, probably after hearing Whitefield speaking of his own visit there. Wesley came to Wales in October 1739, the first of 11 visits in the following seven years. After that, Ireland became the focus of his attention, and Wales was simply a place through which he had to pass on the way. From about 1758 onwards Wesley resumed his visits specifically to Wales, and altogether he visited the country on preaching tours no less than 53 times during his life.

By 1741 the Methodists in England had split into two factions, one being Calvinistic, led by Whitefield, which was to be the more prominent in Wales, Indeed, if you say Methodist in Wales, the general understanding is that you are talking about the Calvinistic Methodists (now also known as the Presbyterian Church of Wales). The Arminian faction, led by the Wesleys, was to be less influential in Wales, and by the time they did become important, they would be referred to as Wesleyans, as the Calvinists had already taken the name of Methodists.

Illustration 2: Howel Harris played a very prominent role in bringing the Methodist revival to North Wales, including Caernarfonshire

By 1742 the Methodist revival had spread throughout Wales, with Howel Harris as the foremost leader, preaching up to seven times a day.

In 1743 PeterWilliams, who was then attending Carmarthen Grammar School, was converted under the ministry of George Whitefield. In 1745 he was ordained as a deacon, but was refused ordination as a curate, and by 1747 he joined the Methodist fold.

Caernarfonshire in the 1740s

We have already described the spiritual state of Wales and England before the Great Awakening of the mid 18th century, and the general situation in Caernarfonshire was just as grim.

Although, as we have mentioned, there were small groups of godly people meeting in the areas around Pwllheli and Clynnog, they do not seem to have made much of an impact on their neighbours, and continued to be concentrated in the areas where they first established themselves during the Propagation. A return made in 1749 shows much the same distribution as in the census taken more than 70 years previously by Archbishop Sheldon.

It can be said that the Nonconformists formed small, closed communities, and were too grateful for the recent relief from penal laws to wish to draw attention to themselves by proselytising among their neighbours. Through the will of Dr Daniel Williams, a Wrexham Presbyterian who died in 1716, funds were available for providing schools for Nonconformists, and such schools were established in Pwllheli and Caernarfon. Conwy, under the influence of its vicar, refused one.

While the Nonconformists tended to keep to themselves, the majority of the population belonged to the Established Church, but their way of life left much to be desired from a moral point of view. Harpists and ballad-singers were always welcome, while strong men and the fighters during fairs were regarded as heroes.

The image of the very respectable "Welsh Sabbath" when pubs were shut, dates from Victorian times, and would be a total anachronism for the 18th century. As soon as the service in the Parish Church ended, the priest would be the first out, and everybody would try to be the first to get to the public house. This would be where the sexton would announce the dates of fairs and markets, lost items that had been found, and where workers were needed. The public house was therefore a major hub of the community.

Marriages and funerals often took place on Sundays, as this was generally the only day when people did not have to work.

Although the people would gather in church to worship in the morning, the Sabbath was not entirely a day of holiness. Afterwards, as decreed in the Book of Sports from the time of Charles I, such games as throwing a ball against the church wall, or football, would be conducted in the churchyard, and even clergy would take an active part in these sports. Yet the churchyard was considered too sacred to allow Nonconformists to read a few Bible verses and to bury their dead.

William Williams, Ceunant Coch, in his book *Hynafiaethau a Thraddodiadau Plwyf Llanberis a'r Amgylchoedd*, (Antiquities and Traditions of the Parish of Llanberis and surroundings), paints a vivid, but bleak picture of the morality that then existed.

He said that after the Sunday morning service, the rest of the day would be spent playing ball games, jumping, fighting and drinking, and often the minister would actually take a leading role in these activities. On Saturday nights the youngsters would entertain themselves with singing, harp music and dancing until the break of the Sabbath dawn. The playing of interludes was very popular, and audiences would travel considerable distances to see had hear these, and they would be announced by the sexton during the Church services. In the evenings the people would meet to tell stories about ghosts, fairies, spells and magic, and other superstitious topics. There was a great belief in dreams, and every unusual happening was taken to be a "sign", with animals being messengers from another world, and the hooting of owls and the howling of dogs being considered as announcing impending deaths.

The situation was similar in the parish of Llanllyfni, where the inhabitants would gather for worship in the morning, but after the service they would play ball games or hold weightlifting contests.

In another part of the parish, the inhabitants would gather on Sundays on a field belonging to a smallholding called Buarthau. The activities taking place there would include cock-fighting, playing crown and pitching, while in a particular corner of the field, old men would exchange tales of the ghosts they had seen during the past week.

There was an old woman in the district, called Gwen y Canu (Gwen of the Singing), who allegedly had the power of putting curses on people. If neighbours quarrelled, one would approach Gwen and pay her to put a curse on the other. When the other discovered that he or she had been cursed, then that neighbour would pay Gwen to take away the curse.

It can be taken that Llanberis and Llanllyfni were by no means unusual, as descriptions of conditions in Anglesey at the same time also reveal a similar level of ignorance and preoccupation with superstitious phenomena.

It might be considered very appropriate, in the light of the seriously needy mission field which met in that field, that the Methodist were to start preaching their message of salvation in Buarthau in the 1760s.

Special days such as the fairs on parish patron saints' days (Gwyl Mabsant) were a particularly bad time drunkenness, which would all too often lead to violence, with fighting, not only with fists, but even with sticks. The Rev Thomas Ellis of Holyhead, in Anglesey, who was certainly no Methodist was very eager to put a stop to these disgraceful scenes.

This was no less the case in Caernarfonshire, as groups from rival parishes sometimes went to the patronal fairs at nearby parishes to fight with the men of that parish.

Robert Thomas, of Ffridd, Baladeulyn, was the chief fighter of Llanllyfni parish. A battle had been arranged between the men of Llanllyfni and the men of Clynnog, at Clynnog's patronal fair, on the Whit Monday, and Robert was to lead the Llanllyfni contingent. He rose early that morning to prepare for the battle, and armed himself with a stick made of oak, and went out while his wife and children wept. They had no idea in what condition he would return, if indeed he would return at all.

He insisted that he would knock down half a dozen of his opponents, and the other half a dozen would be glad to run away.

However, as he reached Capel Uchaf, near Clynnog, he heard singing coming from the house of Edward the tailor. He went in, and felt drawn to join in the worship, and remained there till the end of the worship.

His wife was surprised when he returned, and he explained that a mile before Clynnog he heard singing coming from a house, and there he heard one of those new people preaching, and he had never heard anything like it. As a result, he vowed never to get drunk again, and would never fight again, except against sin and the devil.

Meanwhile, the men of Llanllyfni had found themselves without their leader, and none of them ventured to meet the Clynnog fighters, so the battle had to be postponed. Doubtlessly, many of the Clynnog men must have been secretly relieved at not having to face the giant of Ffridd with his big oak stick.

In such a situation, a visitation of God's Spirit would be badly needed, and the following chapters will relate how this did come about. Incidentally the men in South Wales, about whose conversions we have read in the last chapter, will turn out not to have been irrelevant to this book, as they played a crucial part in bringing Methodism to Caernarfonshire, though it has to be said that their impact on North Wales was less than in South Wales.

Seeds of Awakening

The Methodist revival first reached Caernarfonshire in 1741, and first took root in Llŷn and Eifionydd, the very areas where Puritanism had established itself.

Early in 1741 Howel Harris extended his mission to North Wales for the first time, through the invitation of Lewis Rees, a Montgomeryshire minister who belonged to the wing of Dissent which welcomed the new "enthusiasm".

Harris then continued his journey through Bala and Trawsfynydd, and then across the Traeth to Penmorfa and Llangybi. This was a route that John Wesley would frequently follow a few years later, but Wesley would head north after the Traeth, for Caernarfon, because his objective was Ireland.

The question of why did Howel Harris turn west for Llŷn and Eifionydd is not easy to answer. Many accounts have been offered, but they are all agreed on one point. The invitation came from William Pritchard, a substantial farmer of Glasfryn Fawr, in Llangybi parish. This is the same William Pritchard who later fled to Anglesey to escape persecution, and became known as William Pritchard, Clwchdernog.

Local tradition depicts William Pritchard as an easy-going churchman who was awakened to religious zeal by chancing to pass one night under one of the "country" members of the Pwllheli congregation when family worship was in progress. This made a deep impression; he began to find his vicar's sermons "unscriptural" and to set his heart on a visit from one of Griffith Jones's schoolmasters and from one of the South Wales revivalists.

The former of these aims was achieved first. A Circulating school at Llanuwchllyn in Merioneth had just run its course, and the teacher, Jenkin Morgan, brought the school to Llangybi. This is the same Jenkin Morgan who later kept a school in Cerrigceinwen, Anglesey, and in 1746 became the first Nonconformist minister in Anglesey.

The use of the parish church for the Circulating School had been refused, so William Pritchard accommodated it in his farm kitchen, with both children and adults among the pupils.

It was Jenkin Morgan who went to Bala to accompany Howel Harris to Glasfryn. Harris preached to the Llangybi Dissenters, and during the next five days travelled through Llŷn as far south as Llangian, and as far north as Nefyn and Porthdinllaen, preaching where he could find hearers, sometimes making contact with existing groups of Dissenters, whom he always tried to woo back into the Church. Since the Methodists were still considered themselves an evangelical movement within the Church of England, this would seem logical, although the church authorities were rather suspicious of these more radical churchmen who had affinity with the true Dissenters. It was only in 1811 that this suspicion finally forced the Methodists to separate and become a denomination in their own right.

Howel Harris then returned to Glasfryn and back to Merioneth. He had met with a lot of popular hostility, and with opposition from the civil and ecclesiastical authorities, notably from Chancellor John Owen, the vicar of Llannor and Deneio, who virtually ruled the diocese, and showed great hostility to both the Nonconformists and the Methodists, a hostility that might have been moderated had the Bishop himself (the more tolerant Zachary Pearce) been at hand.

William Pritchard and Jenkin Morgan were both victims of the vicar's fury. The former lost his farm, while the latter was arrested as a vagabond on his way south. Pritchard was also cited before the Church court, where his slighting comments on the vicar's sermons were held against him. This case was carried on to Great Sessions, and dragged on for two years. William Pritchard was a man of means, who could hire a good lawyer, and won his case.

It can be said that this persecution was counter-productive in the sense that this was to drive William Pritchard and Jenkin Morgan to flee to Anglesey. These both renounced Anglicanism, and became Independents, and brought Nonconformity to an area where the Propagation and the Roundhead army had failed to make a lasting impact.

In 1745 William Roberts, the parish clerk of Llannor and a personal friend of the Chancellor, wrote an interlude which was basically a satire on the Methodists.

The hostility to these new preachers may be easily understood, since the nicknames given to them echo the period of the rule of the saints. They were called the Pengryniaid (Roundheads) or Cradocks (after one of the agents of the Propagation).

It was only 80 years before that the houses of local Puritans had been ransacked for arms, and cases of pistols found, and not much more than 30 since Richard Edwards of Nanhoron died, who had served under General Lambert.

To the authorities these preachers who ignored parish boundaries were a threat to Church discipline, while the general population tended to resent anybody who interfered with their sinful pleasures.

Howel Harris was undeterred by this hostile reception. During the next dozen years he made further preaching tours of Llŷn and Eifionydd, sometimes accompanied by other Methodist leaders from the South.

Less than a year after Harris's first visit to Llŷn, there were prosecutions in the Bishop's Court for the holding of "conventicles"(doubtless Methodist Societies) in the Llanbedrog area, and in 1747 charged were brought against inhabitants of Llangian and Llanengan for assembling to hear a "presumptuous strolling person" (almost certainly a Methodist "exhorter").

In that year there were four Societies in Llŷn, with about 30 members.

Local tradition maintains that the terror caused by the partial eclipse of the Sun helped in the spread of Methodism into Arfon, as this happened at about the same time as Howel Harris's visit to Waunfawr. His contacts there were Caernarfon Independents who had taken refuge there from the hostility of the

County town. His advice to them was to return to the Church, in the hope of influencing it from inside with their spiritual zeal.

Before long, the local societies had their own local leaders, and were able to keep going with only occasional visits by evangelists from the South. As early as 1748 a farm hand at Cefnamwlch is said to have undertaken a general oversight of converts in the neighbourhood. Soon afterwards his place was taken by another disciple of Howel Harris, a carpenter called Charles Mark, who became a farmer, and in 1752 built, as an annex to his farm of Ty Mawr (in Bryncroes parish) a tiny thatched meeting house, believed to be the first building in the county to be devoted entirely to Methodist worship. It became a focal centre for the Methodists over a wide area, and Charles Mark remained a pillar of the cause till his death in 1795. A report to the bishop in 1776 declared that half the parishioners of Bryncroes were Methodists.

In 1746, the Caernarfonshire Methodists gained their first convert in the higher reaches of society, during a visit by Peter Williams. This was the mistress of Cefnamwlch herself, the wife of William Griffith, an important man socially, but apparently rarely sober, and often violent at home.

When Harris visited the district again two years later, she accompanied him to the Methodist Assemblies down south, and when her husband refused to have her back, she remained there till her last illness, becoming a cause of bitter dissension among the Methodist leadership, which put a brake to its missionary activities.

In the 1750s it was mainly local zeal, with occasional support from South Wales, which carried Methodism deeper into Eifionydd and Arfon, when two new societies were established, at Brynengan (in Llanystumdwy parish), and just outside Clynnog. Both these areas had been ones where Puritanism had some impact in the 17th century, which might have helped to prepare the ground for the Methodist preachers.

Llangybi had remained one of the main Puritan centres in the county after the Restoration, and the worshippers who met there in secret included some from Clynnog, where Ellis Rowland had ministered in the days after the Propagation.

In 1718, not much more than 40 years after the forcible dispersion of the "conventicle" addressed by James Owen, Richard Nanney had become vicar of Clynnog, where he remained for nearly half a century.

Richard Nanney was an Oxford man, descended from the ancient Merioneth family, and himself a squire in a small way. From early in his incumbency he was a strong supporter of Griffith Jones's circulating schools in his areas.

Before the end of his incumbency he was filling the old pilgrim church with congregations drawn from far and wide and roused to a high pitch of spiritual excitement by his fervent evangelism.

By the 1760s and 1770s Methodism was making its first contacts with the industrial, as distinct from the agricultural elements in the county; first among the quarrymen of Llanllyfni, and then Llanberis. At about the same time Societies were forming in the areas closest to Merioneth, in the hinterland of the Traeth, and Nantconwy, and the eviction of a Methodist farmer by an unsympathetic landlord who banned the use of farm premises for Methodist meetings, was often the first step to penetrating a new area.

The zeal of the Methodists also began to infect the old Dissenters, which for practical purposes means the Independents. Many people were drawn to the Independents rather than the Methodists because they were unhappy about the Methodists' continued adherence to the Church of England.

The stirrings of the revival also affected the Baptists, who had strong roots in South Wales since the days of the Propagation, but had not established in the north. In 1776 a small band of Baptist missioners set out to evangelise the north. After a successful preaching tour, they returned to Llŷn, and preached at Pwllheli and Nefyn before extending their mission to the Conwy Valley. In both areas they established a nucleus of disciples. Their gospel was essentially the same as that of the Methodists, and at first they had the co-operation of the Methodists and the existing Dissenting bodies, and sometimes the hospitality of their chapels. But their insistence on adult baptism by immersion as the visible sign of conversion soon separated them off, and by the 1780s they too were building their own chapels, and their open-air baptisms in streams and tarns often drew even larger crowds than the field preaching of the Methodists.

In 1771 the United Brethren, commonly known as the Moravians, became another element in the religious life of Caernarfonshire. David Mathias, a Pembrokeshire Moravian, obtained leave from his fellow Brethren to take their gospel to Snowdonia. The Moravians differed from the Methodists in that their stress was mystical rather than doctrinal, and their methods involved personal contacts rather than field preaching to the masses.

In Caernarfon, Mathias had to flee from a mob that pelted him with dirt and stones (which was a common experience for revivalists in that town at that time).

He had a warmer welcome in the hill, and with Drws y Coed, Llandwrog as the resident centre, he established a number of small Societies which met in farmhouses in Nantlle, Beddgelert and a far as Criccieth, with one under the friendly roof of John Morgan, the penurious but hospitable curate of Llanberis. This mission lasted only five years, but an attempted come-back in the early 1790s, with a much quieter Caernarfon as its centre, achieved little although it did make a contribution to the general atmosphere of religious revival that swept the county.

One aspect of this was the influence of the Moravian mission in turning John Morgan into a powerful evangelistic preacher, whose preaching drew people from as far as 12 or 15 miles away to listen.

Alongside the religious revival, the educational revival progressed, following much the same path. After Jenkin Morgan's Circulating school had run its course at Glasfryn, the movement extended westwards to the furthest part of Llŷn, where two schools had been set up by the end of the following year. Then the movement spread eastward into Arfon, and by 1750 into Arllechwedd, with the establishment of a school in Llandygai.

By 1761 a total of 85 Circulating schools (the largest number of any county in North Wales) had been set up in Caernarfonshire. These schools did not run concurrently, but did often return to a parish several times within a year or two. The teachers were mostly local curates, and sometimes parish clerks. While the education offered was rather rudimentary, it did facilitate the spread of revivalism by providing the nucleus of literate lay helpers which would be needed to consolidate the work of Methodist leaders.

The settlement of Thomas Charles at Bala meant that Methodists in North Wales, including Caernarfonshire, had a more convenient focal point. The Sunday school, which he helped to establish in North Wales, catered (like the Circulating Schools previously) for adults as well as children, and drew into the Methodist movement many who simply wanted to learn to read and write.

The preaching tours conducted by Thomas Charles gave the Methodist cause a new life, through a succession of mass "revivals", some localised, and some more widespread. The more extravagant phenomena, such as the ecstatic leaping which in 1762 had earned the Methodists the nickname of "Jumpers" became rarer, but shouts of joy and tears of contrition continued to mark the meetings.

Although the effects of these revivals were sometimes ephemeral, there were also lasting and visible fruits, such as the increase in the numbers and membership of Methodist Societies, and the emergence of new evangelists, and during the last decade of the 18th century an increase in church building.

Evan Richardson, a Cardiganshire man, who had been intended by his parents for the Anglican priesthood, was influenced by Daniel Rowland to join the Methodists, and was persuaded by Robert Jones of Rhoslan to open a school at Brynengan on the line of Griffith Jones.

Brynengan became the centrepoint of a widespread revival in Eifionydd. Among his pupils and disciples at Brynengan was Robert Roberts, a former Cilgwyn quarryman who became a powerful lay preacher, with Clynnog as the main centre of his activities.

From Brynengan, Richardson moved to Pwllheli and Llangybi, and afterwards to Caernarfon. His settlement at Caernarfon showed that Methodism had finally overcome this strategic but difficult citadel, and in 1793 a Methodist chapel was finally built in the town.

During the next dozen years the movement spread rapidly along the coast to Bangor, Llanfairfechan and Penmaenmawr, and inland to the quarrying areas of Arllechwedd.

The law that had been invoked against the Methodists was that of Charles II against unlawful conventicles, which had been repealed by the Toleration Act of 1689, but only in respect of registered and licensed congregations of Protestant Dissenters. Thomas Charles now advised his followers to register their chapels under that name, a name which they had studiously avoided. The Methodists in Conwy had already followed this course in 1793, which became a common one in the following century, though sometimes they hedged this by merely using the word "Protestant" which seems to have satisfied the authorities. Sometimes they called themselves "Methodists", and after the Wesleyans had appeared in the county, they would call themselves "Calvinistic Methodists", and their licenses were accepted under that name.

It was getting increasingly difficult for Methodists to avoid the taint of Dissent, or for lay preachers to be satisfied with being allowed to preach but not to administer the sacraments, unlike their Dissenting brethren. As a result, Thomas Charles conferred on eight of these preachers what was in effect Presbyterian orders.

Early Revivals in Caernarfonshire

Caernarfonshre saw a series of revivals from the late 18th century onwards. While the 1735 revival at Llangeitho, like the 1859 and 1904 revivals, were national in their scope (the two latter revivals were international in their scope, affecting several countries), many of the revivals during the late 18th century were local, sometimes covering a single village and its immediate vicinity.

The older Dissenting groups, as well as the Methodists, were caught up in the atmosphere of revivalism. The groups left behind by the Baptist mission of 1775 still had the missionary spirit, and public baptisms have in themselves the elements of a revival meeting. From 1783 the Baptists began to look beyond makeshift arrangements like open-air meetings and borrowed pulpits, and built their own chapels.

Much of their success was due to the tireless evangelism of Christmas Evans, who had educated himself while serving as a labourer, and became one of the shining lights of the Welsh pulpit. From 1789 to 1791 he served as an itinerant evangelist to the Baptists of Llŷn, before moving to look after the churches in Anglesey.

Illustration 3: Christmas Evans was instrumental in establishing the Baptists in North Wales

Revivalism was not in the tradition of the Caernarfonshire Independents, and in the 1740s they had relied on the help of their more active brethren in Montgomeryshire to evangelise, but in 1769 the little group which met at Lon Dywyll in Llangian parish bought a plot of land to build their first chapel, Capel Newydd, which became the missionary centre from which sprang a number of daughter churches.

The Independents in Caernarfon had maintained a degree of continuity since the days of Ellis Rowland, but had no permanent home, and only occasionally had the ministry of a settled pastor. But in 1785 they invited George Lewis to the pastorate. This young man, fresh from the Carmarthen academy, proved to be an eminent theologian and also a man of great evangelical fervour, whose widespread preaching during his nine year pastorate gave new life to the Independents, and it was he that persuaded Mrs Edwards of Nanhoron to bestow land for the first Independent chapel in Caernarfon.

The series of revivals which broke out in Caernarfonshire include the following:

A great revival in Clynnog in 1765.

In 1771 a revival broke out at Salem Calvinistic Methodist church in Llanllyfni. As the number of hearers had grown, it became necessary in 1771 to build a chapel, which was built on land at Buarthau, eight yards in length and six yards in breadth. The people of the region mocked the believers, saying that they would never have half enough hearers to fill it. But not long after, a small revival broke out, which added to the number of hearers, and for the next 22 years, more revival fires kept breaking out, to culminate in a particularly powerful one in 1793, which added many more to the church. There were no further revivals at Llanllyfni from 1796 until 1814, but providentially, a new chapel had been built by then, which was able to accommodate the new hearers.

A revival took place in Capel Uchaf, Clynnog in 1779. It started in a prayer meeting held in the chapel house, and such influences descended on those present that they would never forget it. The following Sunday, Richard Dafydd, a rather ordinary preacher from Llŷn was preaching there. This time he was "clothed with power from on high", and large numbers joined the church in subsequent weeks.

There had been a small Methodist cause at Saethon Bach, Llŷn for some years, and in 1780 a powerful outpouring came on the people there, so many were saved and added. As a result, this meeting place became too small, and Capel y Nant was built in its place (this chapel will play an important part in the start of the Beddgelert Revival of 1817-22).

In 1785 Clynnog had another revival, under the ministry of the crippled Robert Roberts, Clynnog (1762-1802), who was 23 at the time. This anointed preacher had a powerful impact on the life of his own church. The revival spread to nearby Brynengan when he went to preach there, and people of all ages felt the divine grace.

There was a revival among the Baptists in Llŷn, in 1789 under Christmas Evans, who had just taken up his ministry in the area. Revival characterised much of his ministry in the area during 1789-91, and afterwards in Anglesey.

During the 1790s many places in Caernarfonshire had been awakened.

There were several revivals in 1811, but the work at Tŷ Mawr, Llŷn was chiefly among the older people.

The Beddgelert Revival

A wide area of North Wales and parts of the South were impacted by a major revival during 1817-22 which had its epicentre at Beddgelert, and became known as the Beddgelert Revival. This attractive village, which for a long time drew visitors because of its scenery (and from 1798 the legend of Gelert, Prince Llewelyn's faithful hound), for a time drew people who wanted to witness the spiritual effects of the awakening then taking place.

Robert Jones said of this Revival: "Nobody remembers seeing anywhere a more powerful burning of the means of grace than was experienced in this locality and many other places. The convictions were more powerful to awaken the conscience, smiting the heart, and the joy of salvation more powerful than were seen in some previous revivals".

The preparation for the Beddgelert Revival could be said to have started a long time before, as Robert Jones, Rhoslan ran a circulating school in Beddgelert in 1765, his first after he had been trained. Although only there for half a year, he won the hearts of the children, and shared with them some of the stories of the growth of Calvinistic Methodism in Wales, and sowed seeds into some young minds, including Robert Dafydd, who began preaching in 1773 and became the leader of the influential Calvinistic Methodist work at Brynengan. It was he who originally established a strong spiritual link between Brynengan and Beddgelert, which would bear fruit in the great move of the Spirit in 1817.

In 1782 Henry Thomas of Aberglaslyn established a school in Nantmor which met in an old corn kiln. Reading was taught there through the use of the Bible, and hymns were sung. However, the school was forced by opposition from some living nearby to move to an old bark store at Corlwyni, a slightly more remote farm on the mountainside. It was Henry Thomas who invited Robert Dafydd to preach at Nantmor, but he was unable to come, so Robert Jones substituted for him. According to David Jenkins, this was the first time that there had been preaching by Nonconformists in the district, and he described what happened as follows:

As no-one had preached in the district before... the novelty of the service attracted a large crowd, many of whom were bent on a little fun. It was a sore trial to try and preach while a number in the rear of his audience kept laughing, joking, and scoffing. When he had been at it for some time, and was almost downhearted, a terrific storm of thunder and lightning suddenly came on, and both audience and preacher were for a moment mute. Looking at last into the very eyes of the people, he began to use his opportunity in speaking of the thunders of God against every form of ungodliness; and terror fell upon all present. Tender ministrations afterwards led many on the side of faith, from a crisis into which the twofold thunders had driven them.

This event marked the beginnings of the Methodist cause in the area, which a little later moved its meeting place to the home of a solicitor named Hughes at Ty'n y coed, in Cwm Colwyn, just to the north west of Beddgelert. Here the group grew significantly. Several men who would be key leaders in the years that followed joined the cause at this time. The group later met in rented premises in Beddgelert itself, in a house which once stood on the site of the Prince Llewelyn Hotel, just by the bridge over the river.

Beddgelert

Illustration 4: Beddgelert in about 1845, from a print by Hugh Hughes. Courtesy of the National Library of Wales.

However, by the eve of the 1817 Revival, true religion was at a a low ebb in Beddgelert. Barrenness was felt in the means of grace. Older Christians were indifferent, and the young people were worldly. It was a dreadfully ungodly place, with a noswaith lawen (a light concert) every week in one of the taverns, which would result in people getting drunk, swearing, cursing and fighting.

Despite all this, there was a small but faithful community of about 40 Calvinistic Methodists in Beddgelert. According to John Jones, Glan Gwynant, who in 1817 would have been in his mid thirties, and who was one of the members of the group, they had a reputation for their brotherly love and unity of spirit. However, they had not seen any growth through conversion for some years, nor had they received any visits from hearers. This was so much the case, that the place had a reputation among ministers in the north for being a "hard and difficult place".

One tale of the origins of the revival attributes its start to a visit of Williams o'r Wern to Beddgelert in the early years of the 19th century, and an incident in this story accounts for the revival's colloquial name of "Diwygiad y ganwyll ddimai" (The halfpenny candle revival). The surrounding country was in a desperate state of wickedness, and religion was at a discount. Williams o'r Wern, preaching to a sparse audience of the Beddgelert peasantry, advised them to reform both ends of the Beddgelert parish, and then it would not be long before the whole of Beddgelert would come under the elevating influence of the Gospel.

He advised them to do this by holding prayer meetings to ask for the downpour of the Holy Spirit. This appeal was lost on the audience with the exception of one old woman, who had buried the words of the preacher in her heart. About 12 months after this, a deacon called at the old woman, who also kept a small shop. The old woman asked the deacon when they intended to hold the prayer meeting as the preacher had advised. She told him that she had bought two halfpenny candles immediately after the visit by Williams o'r Wern, on the expectation that his advice would be carried into effect, and thinking that her house would be selected as a fitting place for a prayer meeting. But by then the candles had almost been eaten away by mice during the long period of her expectancy. The deacon was impressed by the quaint sincerity of the old dame, and laid the matter before his fellow worshippers, and this led to the Beddgelert revival.

During the winter of 1816, the Sunday School superintendent at Capel y Nant, a few miles north of Abersoch in Llŷn, was concerned about the lack of discipline among the children. He urged them to spend the time available between the means of grace on the Sabbath in prayer that the Lord would visit them by the Spirit. The spirit of prayer and supplication soon characterised the church members as well as the children.

It seems that the public Sabbath meeting was held at 2pm, and the Sunday school was held in the evening. The result was that many of the children remained around the chapel without going home, especially if their home was far from the chapel. During this time there was more than a possibility that they could get into mischief.

However about the beginning of the summer, one of the boys, who had been as bad as any of his contemporaries, started to separate himself from the others and, unknown to everybody else, he would lock himself in the chapel's gallery as soon as the congregation left the afternoon sermon. He was to reveal later that he did this because the polluting of the Sabbath had become painful to him, and he wanted to have quiet from the tumult of the others. This boy was lame, and his home was a long way away, so he could not go home and return in time for the Sunday school.

After a few Sundays, the other children came to understand what was going on, and a girl called Catherine Hughes, after some pleading, was allowed to join the boy in the gallery on condition that she did not make any noise. After that other children also asked to join him, again on the same condition, so that there was a large number of children in the gallery.

No-one outside knew what was going on inside, but those who enjoyed the advantage of being received. This developed into a secret prayer meeting, and gradually, through the amount of their desire, they resolved to come together on an evening in the middle of the week, to hold prayer meetings on a certain furzy slope in the neighbourhood, a place well-known to them, where they would not be seen or heard by anyone.

Calvinistic Methodist churches have monthly meetings, where representatives of local churches would discuss what was happening, and no doubt the leadership of other chapels would have heard of the revival at Capel y Nant through the meeting in January 1817, and one of the representatives present was an elder from Beddgelert. This news would have inspired the Christians of The Calvinistic Methodist church in Beddgelert to pray for a similar revival to come to their area.

Meanwhile, there were small signs that a revival was on its way to Beddgelert itself. Within two weeks the saints at Beddgelert found it easier to enjoy the means of grace as there was a noticeable increase in the power and authority of the preaching. This was followed by further tokens of grace, as in the March, one man came to the Methodist society who had not been before, and during the summer another two or three came. This encouraged the zeal of the faithful, but this was by no means a full-blown revival.

The actual revival was to break out during a preaching meeting on a Sunday evening in August at a farmhouse in another part of the parish of Beddgelert. Richard Williams, Brynengan, was preaching at the old farmhouse of Hafod y Llan, in Nant Gwynant, two or three miles north of the village, with such a powerful effect that some people cried out in view of their conviction, while others rejoiced.

Inhabitants of the surrounding brooks and valleys and the village gathered at the old farmhouse of Hafod y Llan, but the crowds gathered more because the weather was pleasant, and that it was a convenient opportunity to meet each other, than to hear the preacher. Richard Williams was considered a very ordinary preacher.

The kitchen at the old farmhouse, where the preacher and his congregation were, was full that evening, while the young and thoughtless withdrew to the milking parlour, to be out of view, since they were uninterested in the meeting in the kitchen. Richard Williams stood on a bench by the large table in the kitchen. A small table on the large table served as a form of pulpit to hold the Bible.

At the beginning of the meeting the audience seemed disengaged and not particularly interested. Richard Williams preached on John 6 v 44: "No man can come to me unless the Father draws him, and I will raise him up on the last day."

But within 15 minutes of the beginning of the sermon the fire of God fell. Although Richard Williams was preaching, yet it seemed as if it was not his voice, nor his sermon. He had preached on this text before, but this was a completely new sermon, and the effect on the was more than mere fluency. He was a messenger this time, and it was someone else that was speaking to the conscience of the congregation. Even the preacher himself said afterwards that he was doubtful at the time whether he was preaching, or whether he was listening to someone else.

Certainly, everyone had been possessed by seriousness and fear. The young people and the wanton left the milk parlour, taken with fear of the judgement; they thought that an angel and not a man was speaking. The remarkable thing is that the crowd had been possessed by too much fear to weep. After the service everyone was possessed with too much seriousness to sing, and hurried away in quietness and fear. No one said a word to anyone else along the way as they made their way home, nor when they had gone, but what was necessary. This was a sleepless Sunday night for some, and there was grave silence the following day because of their concern over matters of the soul.

Sometime in the following week, a church meeting was held in the village. Although there were three places for preaching, there was only one church meeting, and that was during the day. The "seiat profiad" (experience meeting) had not yet been moved to the night.

Two elders came to this meeting, and when they saw the great numbers waiting to come in they thought that they must have been mistaken, and were expecting a sermon rather than a seiat. Only a handful would usually gather for the seiat, but this time the church was full of people, and not necessarily the kind who would be expected at a seiat.

However, there was nothing to be done but to get one of the brothers to start the meeting. Someone read a portion of the Bible, and then a verse was given to sing. During the singing of the verse, the dams of emotion broke out, The chapel was full of people who were at an end of themselves, and the stirred feelings and tumult within needed an entrance to break out, and the verse given presented the idea of hope. This resulted in an amazing scene where some cried out for mercy, while others rejoiced at having received deliverance, some sang and some sang. Everything was in confusion, with nobody thinking or caring about order. The news of the stirring in the chapel immediately went around the village, and from house to house, and valley to valley, so that everyone hurried to the place, and fell into the grasp of the same exciting influence.

An account published in 1878 describes what happened:

What followed was amazing! Some crying out for mercy – some rejoicing having received deliverance – some praying – some singing – everything in confusion – no one caring – no one thinking about order! Order indeed; under such powerful influences as these!... The news of the stirring in the chapel immediately went through the village, and from house to house – from valley to valley through the region, and everyone hurried to the place, and everyone fell into the grasp of the same exciting influence. Late in the day, or rather late at night, some of the wisest succeeded in guiding their most stirred companions homeward. Now the rejoicing that was in the chapel spread in different directions, along the ways, and through the valleys. The echo of the rejoicing was also taken up by age old Snowdon, one rock competing to answer the other. It was a new and strange work for these ancient everlasting rocks to have opportunity to have a part in praising their Creator! The like was not had again! There was for a period of time hardly any order, nor a seiat or preaching kept, for the praying or singing would start to set everyone on fire. And if leisure was had to start preaching, if the preacher was not watchful of coldness, he would not have quiet to finish his sermon, so fiery were the feelings of the congregation."

Within a few weeks almost every home in the Nant Gwynant area had been touched by the power of God, with many of the people joining with the Methodist meeting place in Beddgelert.

The next notable incident tool place in a Sunday School meeting in Beddgelert on September 14, 1817, when the young women in one of the classes were moved to tears while reading a portion of St John's Gospel.

A young religious girl was the teacher of a number of young girls. As the last chapters of John were being read, a remarkable weeping came upon them all. They could not proceed with their reading for weeping.

At the end of the meeting, Richard Roberts of Cae'r Gors, superintendent of the Sunday School, addressed the whole Sunday school. This brother had a prodigious talent and affectionate manner. At the end of the address, he warned the young people to behave themselves in a seemly manner in a fair that was to take place in Beddgelert the following Sunday, and avoid coming under its influences of worldliness, and immorality. While speaking, something amazing descended on him and the whole school. He came across the line of an old verse by William Williams, Pantycelyn, "Mae'r afael sicraf fry!" (The firmest hold is above). And with his flexible gift and burning feeling, he played on the word "above". "From above comes everything of worth to this world of ours – from above comes light, heat and rain – from above comes the blessings of salvation to our world – from on high God pours out his spirit; here is hope for the hard men of Beddgelert. If it is dark here, it is light above; if it is feeble here, it is strong above." With his words something so solemn, so powerful, descended on the whole school, on young on old, so that all were overcome by the sense of God's presence.

Some of the old believers began leaping and rejoicing, and others cried out, asking "What shall we do to be saved?"

So powerful was the influence, that the children were in dread; one little boy ran to his father, and cried, "Dear father, judgement day has come. A serious and quiet weeping filled the place. There was only one youth who did not have some manifest working of the Spirit upon them.

An unusual phenomenon which came to be associated with this revival was "singing in the air" which John Jones claims was reported by many reliable witnesses. This seems to have consisted of the sound of heavenly angelic voices, sweetly and softly joined in harmony, without any apparent melody, which was overpowering. The effect on the hearer was to render him incapable of movement, as though nailed to the spot. The emphasis on reliable witnesses is important, because there were sceptics who denied that such an occurrence could possibly happen. Richard Williams, Brynengan relates at least two occasions when sceptics heard this singing very soon after ridiculing the idea, and were no longer able to deny it.

By Christmas 1817, the revival had spread to some of the surrounding valleys, particularly to Nantmor, to the south of Beddgelert (so according to William Williams o'r Wern's prophecy, both ends of the parish had been reached).

It was at Tylyrni, a small farm at the bottom of Cwm Nantmor, which was one of the main centres of Calvinistic Methodist preaching in the area, that the first incidence of "singing in the air" was recorded. While it was never determined what exactly was the cause of this singing, some think that it was the angels singing and rejoicing.

Griffith Pritchard, who was aged about 17, lived at Tylyrni with his parents, and on Christmas Eve, 1817, he and his sister kept house, while his parents were out. At about 9pm he happened to go to the window, and there he suddenly heard the sound of a host of voices. At first he though that he understood the words of the singers, but soon realised that was not actually the case. He was overcome by the sweetness of the music, and could not say long how long it lasted, but it glided slowly overhead, and then faded away as it went away, until it became inaudible beyond Llanfrothen. When his parents returned, he asked them whether there had been much rejoicing at Beddgelert that evening, and whether anything extraordinary had happened, They assured him that nothing unusual had happened, and then he related to them the story of "the invisible choir."

"The revival," shouted one of them, "the revival is coming to Nanmor!"

The day after the mysterious heavenly singing was first heard by Griffith Pritchard, it was Christmas Day. Edward Jones from Cardiganshire was preaching at Tylyrni that day, and the service was being conducted by David Jones of Beddgelert. There was a strong sense of God's presence that came as he prayed. While he was engaged in prayer, a crowd of people from Beddgelert approached, singing one of the favourite hymns of the revival, and the audience felt something lifting it away from its surroundings. The preacher was soon in the spirit, and his every sentence seemed to pierce the very hearts of his audience. A certain magnetism drew the scoffers from the doorway, and placed them gazing into the preacher's face, and made them drink in every word as ifeir very existence depended on them.

Not long afterwards, on the second Sunday in the New Year, Richard Williams, Brynengan, the man who was used to start the revival with his preaching at Hafod y Llan, was to preach at Tylyrni, and bring conviction through the working of the Spirit. His sermon that morning, on the text of Hebrews 11 v 7, was tremendous in its power and results, that many of the hearers were heard to shout aloud that the door of the ark was being closed against them and that all their hopes were gone.

It seems as if after preaching at Hafod y Llan, Richard Williams himself had bee transformed by the power of the Spirit, so that he was operating on a new level.

Preaching was the prominent feature of the Beddgelert revival. In some revivals the prayer meeting was the greatest feature, and in others it was singing, but preaching was certainly the keynote of the Beddgelert Revival.

This revival was spread in two ways. Many people from all over North Wales, and even parts of England, had heard about the revival, and so came in the hope of "catching the fire". Local people who had been impacted by the revival, also went to nearby districts, which they felt needed to be touched by God's power.

There were many wonderful stories of the encounters with God that resulted from this revival, which are worth retelling.

John Jones, Glan Gwynant, experienced the revival at first hand, and wrote an account of the revival in Goleuad Cymru in 1823, and includes the following description of one sovereign conversion:

"About that time, a remarkable thing happened to one girl as she was milking one of the cows. Some scripture came to her mind with such light and power that she had to cry out where she was, and she cried after she returned to the house, to the great surprise of the family as they heard and saw her. After this she experienced much of the joy of salvation; and until now has cheerfully continued with the work.

Henry Hughes, Bryncir, gives the same story in a book that he published in 1906 about Welsh revivals, and adds that the young girl, whom he described as both very beautiful and intelligent, and until that point was an outspoken critic of the revival. He identifies her as Alice Griffiths, who later married William Griffith Williams. She died in her mid forties, but in spite of dying relatively young, she nevertheless was considered a "mother in Israel" as a result of the extent and quality of her serving in Bethania after her conversion, which seems to have happened when she was about 21 years old.

Robert Ellis tells of a son and daughter who had feasted extensively of the delicacies of the House of God the previous day, and were coming together in a cart to the village. While talking together about religion, they were inspired to praise the Lord, which they did for four miles without ceasing. This man, called Richard Williams, later became a famous elder in Horeb, Prenteg.

Another anecdote recorded by Robert Ellis says that Richard Roberts of Cae'rgors, Beddgelert, at the time when the revival was at its height was in the yard taking care of the haystack when they were carrying in the hay. At one time he was on top of the haystack and looking towards the Meadow when he saw the group in the hay field throw their rakes up in the air, and started rejoicing and leaping with all their might, They had been singing a verse from a hymn that translates as follows:

Jesus is completely lovely, Yes, it's true; Than all the world more worthy. Yes, it's true. My heart is won by Jesus, So farewell, you dumb idols; his face so fair and gentle, Yes, it's true. An ocean wide of comfort, Yes, it's true.

Edward Parry (1845-1926), the Baptist minister of Aberdulais, in 1898 in his book, Llawlyfr ar Hanes y Diwygiadau Crefyddol yng Nghymru, commented as follows on this incident:

"It was not easy to persuade them to focus on the hay they were harvesting. There was more of heaven upon them than anything else. The world was completely forgotten as they were caught up in the spirit of religion; most other people caught in the spirit of the world would simply continue to carry the hay without thinking anything about religion. Many rejoice in the things of the world, but have totally forgotten their religion; and there is nothing that can reverse the order but the influence of the Spirit of God in a religious revival."

The revival had the effect of doubling or trebling Methodist membership, and brought up new leaders, including John Jones, Talysarn, who in 1821 started preaching and was discovered to have outstanding preaching gifts.

Illustration 5: The preaching gifts of John Jones, Talysarn, came to the public's attention through the Beddgelert revival.

During the three years that followed the outpouring of the Spirit during the preaching at Hafod y Llan, there was a great increase in the membership of the church at Beddgelert, which grew from 40 to over 200, at a time when the population of the small mining community was less than 800.

Caernarfon Revival 1832

This revival was touched off by a remarkable sermon of John Elias at the Calvinistic Methodist Association at Pwllheli in September 1831, where he was preaching on Psalm 68 v1, "Let God arise, let His enemies be scattered..."

Having faithfully described the low condition of the church, and having demonstrated unmistakably that God's presence and power were withdrawn from His people at that time, he urged Christians to give themselves to earnest and importunate prayer that God would again arise and visit Zion.

The congregation was overcome with feelings of grief at this description of their state, and yet rejoiced that God could still scatter His enemies.

The fact that this was very soon after the sinking of the Rothesay Castle in a ferocious storm off Beaumaris on August 17, 1831, with only 21 survivors out of the 130 on board, meant that there was a sense of the fragility of human life.

This awareness of mortality became even more heightened later by the cholera epidemic, which had broken out in Western Europe in 1831, and had reached the North of England by 1832. The sobering effects of this epidemic became more acute as it spread through Flintshire and Denbighshire, and by July 1832 had caused 30 deaths in Caernarfon alone.

In 1832, Brynengan was among the first localities to be blessed with a mighty revival, and this was particularly pleasing with the Calvinistic Methodist preacher, Robert Dafydd, who had been instrumental in establishing the strong spiritual link between Brynengan and Beddgelert, which facilitated the revival of 1817.

lHe had been praying for some years before 1832 that God would grant him the privilege of seeing yet one more revival (he died on April 17, 1834, at the age of 87, so this revival came just in time).

His prayer was answered, and the whole of Caernarfonshire felt the impact of an extraordinary manifestation of divine power. As a result, over 600 were added to the church, apart from a considerable number of children.

About the same time, Llanystumdwy held its Sunday School Jubilee, and the revival broke out in the midst of those present with great power. Some 50 converts became members of the church within a short time, but the revival did not spread to other areas for quite a few months.

1840s Revivals

The Merioneth Revival of 1839-42 started in North Wales and among the Welsh of Liverpool, and spread over practically the whole of Wales, and had been influenced by the writings of two American Revivalists, Charles Finney and Calvin Colton.

In 1832 Colton wrote The History and Character of American Revivals, which argued that revivalists had deliberately preached in such a way as to create hysteria in their audiences. He therefore claimed that non-spiritual factors could be used to hasten revivals.

Revivalists could either use psychological pressure to create the right preconditions, or use external events to create a pathological fear and a sense of unease among the congregation (epidemics, which bring a heightened awareness of mortality, would be a good example of this).

This revival had been inspired by the publication in Welsh of Finney's 1835 publication, *Lectures on Revival*. This book argued that a revival was not just a supernatural invasion by God's presence into a community, but an event that could be created by the correct use of a number of techniques, such as protracted meetings, direct preaching that appealed more to the emotions than to the intellect, and the "anxious seat" at the front of the church where the penitent were encouraged to sit, and where they could be subtly pressured into making a decision. As a result, this revival was a highly organised, and even mechanical.

The application of Arminian principles (on the lines of Finney's methods), and the lack of marked emotional agitation have led some to argue that it did not truly qualify as a revival, but on the other hand comparatively few people fell away afterwards, which indicates that it was a true revival.

The influence of Finney's methods gave it the nickname of "Diwygiad Finney" (Finney's Revival), though older people more often referred to it as "Y Diwygiad Distaw" (The Quiet Revival), no doubt because they were familiar with the greater excitement and extravagance of previous revivals.

Williams o'r Wern was particularly influenced by Colton's teaching, and placed a great emphasis on revivals in his own churches. Williams was very important in the revival of 1839-40, and introduced the idea that revivals should be actively encouraged.

While there was the motivation of wanting to save souls, there was also the realisation that chapel debts needed to be cleared, which gave a more materialistic motive for wanting to see converts. Within a few months the Independents had collected £18,000 towards a debt of £34,000.

After 1842 there seemed to be a period of declension all over Wales, without almost any revivals for a period of seven years, until 1849, when the outbreak of cholera in market towns and industrial centres, especially in South Wales caused people to seek God's face. Anglesey and Caernarfonshire were also among the areas blessed with this powerful revival in 1848-49, which was characterised by prayer above anything else.

1859 Revival

By 1859 the Churches had declined to an alarming state of deadness and barrenness. The means of grace had become more or less a formality, made unattractive to the world by the coldness of its orthodoxy. Sinful practices were rampant, and carried on without any sense of shame. Prayer meetings were no longer burdened over the lost. The preaching was theoretical and oratorical, but while the churches were generally orthodox in their beliefs, they were ineffective in their witness. Caernarfonshire was no exception to this rule of most of the churches being in a rather moribund state.

However a revival had already been occurring in America, and in June 1858 the revivalist Humphrey Jones, a native of Cardiganshire, who had been instrumental in the American revival, returned to his native county. The spreading of the revival in Cardiganshire heightened the desire already present in the rest of Wales for the revival to come.

Meanwhile the Rev David Morgan, a pastor at Ysbyty Ystwyth, Cardiganshire, was sceptical of the reports of revival, and went to hear Humphrey Jones's revival meeting, to assess its validity, but became convinced that the move was indeed of God, and became aware of the shortcomings of his own ministry.

David one night went to sleep, and woke up early, aware that some mysterious change had come over him. All that that he had ever learned or heard of a religious nature, he could now remember effortlessly. This added keenness of his memory became proverbial while the flames of the revival continued to burn. He could remember the names of everyone he had spoken to, which helped with his intercessory prayers. But less than two years later, this extraordinary supernatural gift was revoked as suddenly as it had been given.

The initially sceptical Rev David Morgan became the major instrument of the revival in Cardiganshire, replacing Humphrey Jones.

In October and November 1859, David Morgan went to Anglesey and Caernarfonshire to preach revival, but it must be said that there were already signs of the Lord's visitation there long before then, as during April and May 1858, even before Humphrey Jones returned from America, there were already remarkable awakenings taking place in Wales.

Two major sources for this chapter are *The '59 Revival in Wales*, written by J J Morgan and published in 1909, the Revivalist's son, and therefore based largely on the Revivalist's experiences, and *The Welsh Revival and its development* by the Rev Thomas Phillips of Hereford, published in 1860. The latter was published so soon after the Revival as to be practically contemporaneous, and contains many eyewitness accounts.

In certain areas, such as Llanfairfechan, Aber and Penmaenmawr, there had been signs of revival long before David Morgan visited North Wales.

At Llanfairfechan the awakening started with the Wesleyans, who in January 1858 had only 24 members. The church decided to be more at the throne of grace and to make the district the subject of prayer. A series of special preaching meetings was held from Monday to Thursday and strong impressions were felt, becoming more irresistible as the work went on.

During the Sundays that followed, the Spirit's influences were overpowering. All present would weep unashamedly, many crying out for mercy, and others praising God for the blood of Christ. By March, 134 had been accepted into membership after inquiry into their spiritual convictions. The Calvinistic Methodists also partook of the blessing, and in the same period 60 were added to their church.

In the year 1858 about 280 persons were added to the two denominations in the Llanfairfechan, Aber and Penmaenmawr area and in 1860 these, with very few exceptions, were still pillars in the church.

The revival spread to neighbouring towns and villages, such as Conwy, Llandudno, Aber, and even as far as Pwllheli.

The revival also helped to fill the Congregational chapel at Ebenezer (now known as Deiniolen). Thomas Edwards had been inducted as minister of the Congregational cause there in July 1832, but five years passed before he saw any appreciable success in his ministry. In 1837 a powerful revival broke out in the church and many were converted. A new chapel was opened in May 1851, which Thomas Edwards feared would be too large for it ever to be filled. In 1858, however, another visitation of divine power dispelled his doubts, as many were again added to the church. Nevertheless, looking back on this work in 1859, he said: "The revival of last year was only like John the Baptist intimating that one stronger than he was at hand."

These instances of local revivals show the longing in some quarters for an effective remedy to a situation that was already alarming, and which showed signs of gradual deterioration.

Prayer meetings started at Hermon Calvinistic Methodist church in Mynydd Llandygai when they heard reports of the revival in America, but after a while the interest diminished, until the Revival had reached Cardiganshire, which rekindled their enthusiasm.

A correspondent to the Drysorfa in December 1859 gives the details:

"Having heard of the great upheaval which had taken place in the courts of Zion's daughter in America, when the saviour's cause was raised, as it were, from death to life there, it came to the mind of the Lord's people in this place to hold a meeting for prayer once a week; and the particular subject of the prayers was to plead that God would also visit them in the influences of His Spirit, as comforter and convicter. This meeting was quite popular for a while; but somehow or other it gradually diminished, until the attendance at the gatherings was very low".

Here also the prayer-meeting received new life upon hearing of the revival in Cardiganshire, increasing considerably in sense of earnestness and urgency as the revival came geographically closer.

The dawn finally broke in the young people's Sunday night prayer meeting, where, under the influence of the Spirit, some prayed for deliverance, while others wept bitterly, and others praised God for having at last visited His people. This went on for some hours, and proved to be the first fruits of a mighty awakening which soon spread to neighbouring churches.

Weekly prayer meetings had been started at Nantmor, near Beddgelert since April 1858. This shows that God was preparing His church for the mighty manifestation of His Spirit, and that the Church was becoming more and more aware of the need for revival, which was born of prayer.

By late 1858 and the beginning of 1859 prayer meetings for revival were held in many places, including Llandudno and Caernarfon. There were a number of causes for these otherwise isolated cases of preparation for the revival, but generally the procedure was governed by local conditions.

By March of 1859 many Calvinistic Methodist churches were being awakened, including at Edern, Jerusalem (Bethesda) and at Pwllheli. At Pwllheli the church had been stirred before the visit of Robert Williams for the March preaching festival. Fifteen were added to the church at that time, and by the end of April, the number of converts had increased to over 100. The number of converts became fewer towards the end of May, but in early 1860 there was a second wave of blessing, and by the end of that year there were nearly 400 converts.

Prayer meetings commenced at Trefriw and Betws-y-Coed in June 1859, but they did not experience the full tide of blessings until October.

Many places in Caernarfonshire experienced powerful movements on Sunday, August 21. "On Monday morning the amazing news was blazed abroad that overpowering spiritual forces had descended the previous evening on every congregation in the neighbourhood." The effects at Llanddeiniolen continued unabated for some months, and were keenly felt, particularly among the young people, the prayer meetings being abundantly used as a means of blessing. Over 100 had been added to the churches there and at Cefn y Waun by January 1860.

The prayer meeting at Bwlan, Llandwrog,in late September 1859 felt overpowering influences which broke out into general outbursts of jubilation and rapture at the young people's prayer meeting on Sunday Night, September 25, and spread from there to neighbouring villages.

Children played a leading part in bringing the revival to certain places such as Llanllechid, Dinworwic and Bangor.

In many cases the young people held prayer meetings of their own, and these sometimes proved instrumental in bringing the powerful influences of the revival to that particular locality. Such was the case at Hermon, Mynydd Llandygai.

It was a young quarryman from Betws-y-Coed who lit the spark which caused an outburst of rapture at Ffestiniog in October 1859. In the meantime 500 had been added to the churches there so the fuel was already dry for a blaze, but there were no manifestations of open rapture and praise, until then.

David Rowland, a preacher from Bala found this young man on his knees at Gorddinen (which is now known as the Crimea Pass) at early dawn on Monday, and passing by a farmhouse, he shouted to the tenant:

"Look out; it's coming!"

"What is coming?"

"The Revival," answered the old preacher.

On the Tuesday morning William Jones from Betws-y-Coed wandered restlessly about the quarry, exchanging experiences with the pious, and warning the wicked, until at last he had infected the whole quarry with his own spirit. The work was disrupted as the men began to pour up the hillside to pray. The quarry was soon emptied, and a second quarry, which heard the news, was likewise emptied of all its men.

One evening a number of quarrymen from Dolwyddelan who were working at Ffestiniog were at a prayer meeting in a little chapel near their home. The chapel was crowded and every male in the congregation was engaged in prayer in succession.

They refreshed themselves after leaving with a cup of tea, but passing the chapel, they discovered that another prayer meeting had been started, and were drawn in. Once again they started homeward towards Ffestiniog, but by the Roman Bridge they entered a cow shed, and held another service of praise and supplication. Here the local friends left them but half a mile farther on they held another prayer meeting beneath the trees at Hafod.

At the Crimea Pass they kneeled together once again to pray, in the cold midnight air on the mountain. Then, after a sixth prayer meeting, one of them left the others as the dawn reminded him that he was due at the quarry in an hour.

The feebleness of Christ's cause at Trefriw made the enemy scoff, but there were a few who continued to be grieved for the affliction of the Lord's people. One Saturday night they were awed by a new and strange note in their devotions, for they knew that it was not something that had come from themselves. They parted saying: "He hath put a new song in our mouth."

The following day's preacher was one of the "great unknown".

"Make bare Thine arm, O Lord," prayed one brother. "We know that the sleeve is only homespun cloth this morning, but what does that matter?"

One of the hearers went out weeping and on the road in front of the chapel he burst into a great and exceeding bitter cry, "O my precious soul! My precious soul!"

His outcries continued till he came home; and in the after-meeting that night he testified "God has saved me; He has saved me at the eleventh hour."

This last intimation puzzled his friends, for he was hale and comparatively young; but manifestly the shadows of the Divine purpose had fallen over his soul, for the record on his tombstone is "Aged 34 years."

A very interesting Revival took place in Llanfairfechan and the neighbourhood early in 1858. There are no grounds for connecting it in any way with the American movement taking place at the same time, which had already attained considerable proportions. It seems to have sprung spontaneously from the religious instincts of God's people, face to face with a crisis in the situation of the kingdom of God amongst them; for Belial was waxing stronger and stronger, and the house of God weaker and weaker.

They realised it was time to supplicate the Lord for reinforcements. One of the united prayer meetings that took place at the time was later to be referred to as "the mute prayer meeting". Five men went successively to offer prayer, but not one of them was able to utter a single word. The audience dispersed, filled with strange feelings, some to pray by the roadside dykes, others in the fields and on the mountains. Before the end of the year nearly 300 souls had been saved from the kingdom of darkness.

The next instance traced of Revival manifestations in Caernarfonshire, at Waunfawr, is clearly linked to the upheaval in Cardiganshire for early in 1859, one of the members received a series of letters from a friend in Llechryd, Cardiganshire, delineating the course and character of the work in that county; and these letters were read in prayer and church meetings to a brotherhood that welcomed such good news from a far country as thirsty souls welcome cold waters.

It was during the Whitsuntide Festival that the Lord rent the heavens and came down, the flinty mountains of age-long indifference and selfishness flowing down at His presence. Before the Revival, it was as difficult to bring a young man to his knees as to drag the "devil to the cross," as one old pilgrim put it. "Now they pray in chapel, at home,. In the rocks, and in the old tunnels of the quarries."

When the Revival flood ran strong, only one resident dared visit a public house by daylight. Six of the converts became deacons. The chapel was rebuilt, enlarged, and opened in 1864,. when the Revival fervour was still unspent.

August 21, 1859 was a memorable Sunday in the Llanddeiniolen district. On the Monday morning the amazing news was blazed abroad that overpowering spiritual forces had descended the previous evening on every congregation in the neighbourhood; those of Cefnywaun, Ebenezer (now called Deiniolen), Dinorwic, Sardis, Rhydfawr, Rehoboth and Llanrug, as an earthquake shock might simultaneously affect a group of villages in a territory three miles square.

After this, whenever one might go abroad, he would hear the rocks redoubling songs and supplications to the hills, and then to heaven. One man said that he was going through Llanrug at 3am, and was surprised to find the chapel lit up, and went in to find a congregation white-hot with flaming "rapture", like a bush that burned with fire and was not consumed.

Religion had fallen on evil days at Bangor, but there was a remnant who redeemed the time. Hearing how the Lord was showing His greatness and mighty hand at Cefnywaun, some of them went over to see if these things were so, and finding that the half had not been told them, were filled with a godly jealousy that Bangor might be baptised with the same baptism.

One of the first converts, named Thomas Jones, said that he had never succeeded in shaking off the influence of a sermon he had heard 40 years before from Daniel Jones, Llanllechid, on the words "If the ungodly will not turn, He will whet His sword...". He indulged for a whole fortnight in a drunken carouse, but the spark of conviction was not to be drowned, though he forgot everything except Daniel Jones's text. After these 40 years the Word of God prevailed.

A veteran saint expressed in a church meeting his delight that so many were asking the way to Zion, with their faces thitherward. It had been a dreary task for years to stand in the house of the Lord by night; but the Revival had brought the morning. In his prayer the same evening Thomas Jones said: "The friends have been grumbling, Lord about standing in Thy house by night; it strikes me that they were very well off to be in the house at all – to stand by night on the devil's common was the terrible thing."

It was arranged to hold the North Wales Quarterly Association at Bangor on September 12-14, 1859. On these occasions the services of one or two gifted preachers from the other end of Wales are generally secured.

"Are you expecting any stranger to the Association this year?" asked an Anglesey man.

"Yes," was the reverent answer of a Bangor citizen, "we are expecting the Holy Spirit."

At 8am on the Tuesday, the preachers held a conference at which they discussed the Revival in an unconstrained way.

About 700 souls were added in a few days to a dozen or so churches. Among them were many who were leaders in iniquity. Old Christians had renewed their youth like the eagle, and the children of the Church had received a special refreshing. The youth of the church, before the Revival, gave no indication of possessing the power of godliness; they were growing up callous in spirit, and would not tolerate rebuke or advice. But now, behold! They pray in their families and in public meetings till all around are weeping. They are now gentle and easily entreated. Before, intemperance was daily gaining ground, but now nearly all the drunkards of the districts have been sobered at a stroke; religion has dethroned impiety in all the neighbourhoods. Those who have watched the results of the Revival are compelled to say, in Christ's words, "The blind receive their sight, the lame walk, the lepers are cleansed"; those who had been ostracised from all decent society because of their vices have become fellow-citizens with the saints; yea. "the dead are raised"; in many a district there were miserable creatures buried in graves of lust, and all who passed by cast a stone on their grave – now the cairns have been scattered, the graves are empty and the dead alive.

In a crowded prayer meeting at Hirael during the Quarterly Association there was an outburst of "rapture" that lasted till the lamps were extinguished at midnight, and many paraded the streets till dawn, singing hymns and "rejoicing".

The sound of approaching rain was heard in the breeze at Dinorwic about August 21, 1859. The children began to slip furtively into the woods to pray. On the following Thursday morning, robust youths in the quarry were seen weeping freely with heads bowed over their work. At 10am a prayer meeting was held at a place called "The Smoky Hole". Instead of providing an escape-valve, this made the weight of emotion intolerable, and the quarry poured itself out and up the slopes of Elidir to relieve the strain. Three would be found kneeling behind this stone, five in this hollow, ten beneath yonder precipice. The mountain burned with the spiritual fire, and guilty souls heard the sound of a trumpet and the voice of words. Many such, who had followed the praying throng either to mock or from curiosity, were overcome by the terrors of Sinai, and, prostrated on the ground, they wildly clutched the short mountain grass, like men in imminent peril of slipping over some appalling precipice. By and by God instilled His peace into their hearts, and they participated in the feast which the Lord of Hosts had spread in that mountain – a feast of fat things full of marrow and of wine upon the lees. They all returned to their burdens in the quarry at about 2pm, but other troops from the village and district took their places, feasting, as it were, on the fragments that were left, and finding enough and to spare until daylight faded.

Another prayer festival was held on the heights of Elidir on September 1, when 3,000 worshippers gathered.

The Bethesda quarry district was described by one writer of the period as a place where religious carelessness and callousness had attained their climax before the 1859 revival. Troops of youths loafed about on the Sabbath who jeered at all reproof and could not blush. The cause of temperance was under an eclipse, and church members were, too generally, hand-in-glove with the world. It was about the beginning of September that the Lord drew nigh to break the gates of brass though it was October before the churches, as a whole, were led into liberty and joy. Throughout the first week in October the prayer meeting was as a river whose streams made glad the city of god, and on the Saturday night it broke in a crystal flood over the banks.

There were two large Calvinistic Methodist chapels in Bethesda at this time – Carneddi and Jerusalem. The same minister officiated in both on Sunday, October 9, preaching at the former in the morning, and the latter at night. That night 16 young men sat on the railing of a bridge, waiting for the opening of the public house door opposite. One of them suggested going to hear Evan Williams, Morfa Nefyn,. At Carneddi, another proposed that they should toss up to decide between the tavern and the chapel. The die being cast, it fell to the lot of eight to go to chapel. They went, and the eight were saved in that service.

The text was "The wages of sin is death, but the gift of God is eternal life." The preacher compared the verse to the pillar in the wilderness, which presented a dark side to the Egyptians and a bright side to the Hebrews. He portrayed with startling vividness the dark side which the text showed to the ungodly, "The wages of sin is death".

The audience felt that it had been brought to the mountain that might be touched, unto blackness and darkness and tempest; and so terrible was the sight that the most hardy and defiant exceedingly feared and quaked. When the preacher, with the find dramatic skill of a true orator, suddenly turned the shining text of the text on his audience, it leapt wildly to its feet, and the air was rent by an universal shout of joyful relief. The tumult was so great that the church meeting for the reception of converts was postponed to the afternoon. At that service 68 yielded.

The same service was preached at night at Jerusalem; and when the preacher cried, "Don't you want to see me turning the leaf? There is something here besides death – Eternal life!" The morning scene was paralleled, and 28 souls were saved.

In a prayer meeting at Carneddi that week 17 penitents remained, each confessing that he was the chief of sinners. The resident minister exuberantly asked, "Dare we bring so many great sinners to Jesus Christ at the same time?"

"Yes," responded a jubilant voice in the crowd, "He is mighty to save."

Another memorable discourse was that of the Rev John Phillips, Bangor, on "The Barren Fig Tree". As he enumerated the reasons for cutting down the tree, the audience cowered and groaned as if they saw the axe descending on themselves. Each Divine attribute in succession can only recommend "Cut it down." Mercy only has not spoken. "Mercy? Have you any remedy to propose? What shall we do with the barren tree?" A man named Owen Williams leaped up and cried with overwhelming results, "Try blood to its roots!" (Many vineyard keepers believe in the efficacy of this treatment).

Burning with missionary zeal, some young men invaded in the name of God a cottage whose inhabitants were a benighted illiterate old woman and her son Evan, a brutal fighter and a ribald drunkard. The onset resulted in leading Evan in the triumph of Christ, but repeated services seemed to affect his mother no more than morning dew dissolves granite. By and by Evan began to read the New Testament to her, and she astonished the company one evening by asking, "What is this Jesus Christ you've got? He's a rare good sort, it seems to me."

A few evenings later a preacher asked her, "What do you think of Jesus Christ?".

"Indeed, He is a caution," she cordially answered.

"Is that so?"

"Yes, when He could save our Evan."

The Bible became as the sun to Evan, He was heard one evening privately reading the story of Christ before the High Priest. Angrily moved, he jumped up, and stripping off his coat, exclaimed "D-, if I had only been there!"

The old woman, when dying, was asked whom she loved best, and her reply was, "Jesus Christ and Evan."

At this time Queen Victoria visited Bethesda to see the quarries, and the men were given a holiday that they might have leisure to see her Majesty. However, what they did was to use this opportunity by crowding into a series of prayer meetings. Another instance may be given of the influence of the Revival.

A certain bookseller normally sold 150 copies of The Welsh Punch, a humorous journal of the period; but with the Revival, its circulation dropped to vanishing point.

But the Revival itself was not without its humorous incidents. A young fellow, in despair of soul, cried out in one service, "My sins are beyond forgiveness!"

"Stop your twaddle!" said the Rev Morris Jones, locally known as "the old prophet" to him; "your sins by the side of the Plan of Redemption are but like hitching a porridge pot to the stern of a man-of-war."

An obscure Bethesda preacher having moved his congregation mightily in one service, a brother thus alluded to it in the next prayer meeting: "Thank God for the Revival! It is changing 'locals' into 'strangers from South Wales'."

Early in November David Morgan was in Llanllyfni. His ministry was wondrously melting, the emotions of the saints flowing in the wake of his cadences as the ocean follows the moon. He spoke of the "Two Ways," saying that the Narrow Way broadened as it advanced, and that walking it paid gloriously at the terminus. A young man in the audience cried, "It pays on the nail, Mr Morgan."

On the gallery stood "Cyrus", a literary character, who had backslid and denied his Master years before. Today he tasted forgiveness, and cried incessantly, "Tell Peter! Tell Peter!" (Mark 10 v 7).

An old woman of 80 "stayed behind" at Nebo, the preacher being "the old prophet" from Bethesda. As he well knew, she had been a persecutor of God's people, especially of her husband, but now she is abjectly penitent.

"Where is she?" asked the preacher.

"Here on your right," answered a deacon, pointing to her,

"That old thing?" asked Morris Jones, a note of scorn keen as a knife in his voice. "That old thing wants to join the society? How old are you, tell me?"

"Eighty."

"Shame!" exclaimed the stern old man. "You've been the devil's dishclout of 80 years, and now you have the face to offer yourself to Jesus Christ. He won't have her!"

Suddenly the scowling, contemptuous countenance of "the old prophet" broke into a smile, like the sun bursting through a thundercloud, Mercy rejoiced over judgement, and he cried "Yes, He will receive her. 'This man receiveth sinners'. There is no-one in the universe but Him who would receive her."

Owen Humphreys, an octogenarian, turned to God at Nebo. When dying, a friend asked him how old he was. "Four," he faintly whispered.

"You mean 84, of course?"

"No – four," he insisted; "I have only lived four years of my time on earth."

When David Morgan preached at Talysarn, one of the converts was a haulier in the quarries with a reputation for brutality towards his horses, One of the elders remarked, "Robert Williams has come to Christ. The old horses must hear about this, Robert."

David Morgan came to Beddgelert on Tuesday, October 11. There was in this place an ungodly, brazen-faced farmer, who made it his pastime in the house of God to stare God's servants in the pulpit out of countenance, and he often boasted to his boon companions that he had never lowered his eyes before one of them. When the Revivalist ascended the pulpit, his gaze ranged as usual over the congregation; and as a mighty warrior in the onset selects the foeman worthiest of his steel, so his eyes became fixed on this man, sitting in the seat of the scornful. The audience recognised at once that an eye-to-eye struggle had commenced between the preacher and the farmer. The preacher too, recognised that the bold, defiant eye glaring at him must be put to shame as the necessary preliminary of a victory over the audience; and the scorner realised that he must extinguish that rebuking flame burning in the preacher's eye, or lose a reputation confirmed by a hundred contests. It was a singular duel, and for a minute or two the issue was not certain. It was the sword of the Lord that drew first blood; for a minute the farmer's eyelids dropped, but he immediately regained his impious strength, and again lifted his insolent looks to the pulpit. However, the flame in the eye of the man of God was more than flesh could withstand, and the scorner's recovery was only momentary; his heart became as water within him, and a flush of self-contempt covered him. Once again he made a desperate effort to rally, but the ordeal of facing the preacher's frown was too terrible for him. He trembled from head to foot, grew pale, then dropped his forehead on the the seat, and so remained till the service was ended.

"What is your name?" said the Revivalist to a middle-aged man among the penitents.

"John Roberts, Brynmelyn."

"You stuck for many years to the old master. I suppose you got a lot out of him. He gave you many a suit of clothes, I suppose?"

"Never a thread," said honest John.

"Do you expect much from the new Master?"

"It was He who gave me all before," was the reverent reply.

Shortly afterwards he found Mrs Catherine Roberts, Brynmelyn, among the converts, and still another said that she was "Gwen Owens, servant at Brynmelyn."

"You Brynmelyn folks must have prearranged this for tonight?" said David Morgan. "Had you, Gwen, told your employers that you meant to join tonight?"

"No, sir, I hadn't breathed a word about it, though it had been on my mind for some days."

"And you hadn't told anyone?"

After a slight hesitation she replied, "I had told my Father."

"Oh! You had told your father. And where does your father live, my girl?"

"In Heaven," was the answer. After adorning the doctrine for 12 months, and before her piety had grown cold, Gwen Owens went to live in her Father's house.

From here David Morgan went to Bethania, the cradle of the great Beddgelert Revival. In the after-meeting, the chapel being packed, the deacons were sent around to look if there were any converts. They returned reporting one by the door.

"There is more than one here," said the preacher confidently. "search again."

They did so, but fruitlessly.

"There must be more than one here," he insisted. "Go around again."

This time he was discovered, an old man of 82, who had escaped detection in a secluded corner of the big seat, where he generally sat owing to his deafness.

"Will you begin to hold family worship at once?" asked David Morgan.

"I began a fortnight ago," was his answer.

"Dear me!" cried the preacher. "And an old man of 84 that I received some time ago had begun three weeks prior to his public confession of Christ."

Returning to Beddgelert, the Revivalist had a very powerful evening service.

He had told them at Bethania in the afternoon that many wounded there would drop at night in Beddgelert, and so it befell. A certain young man shouted distractedly, "Oh! Friends, what shall I do?"

"Why didn't you enlist this afternoon at Bethania when you were sober?" said David Morgan to him.

His conviction was so poignant and profound, that it cost him three weeks in bed to get over the physical effects of it.

The floodgates were lifted high in this neighbourhood, and the tide swept gloriously in. The old hymns of the Beddgelert Revival were resuscitated, and they had the dew of their youth on the lips of the 1859 converts.

When David Morgan preached at Moriah, Caernarfon, one of the 21 converts was a sea captain.

"What have you to say?" he was asked.

"Nothing," replied the bluff sailor, "only that I mean to try a new tack for the rest of the voyage."

Speaking of the "Two Ways," the Revivalist said one was very broad at its entrance and very short. The first mile was the counsel of the ungodly, the second, the way of sinners; the third, the seat of the scornful. The other was very narrow at its entrance and also short; the first mile, out of self; the second into Christ; the third, into glory. Having touched the words, "I will sup with him," he said: "The flesh gives a man breakfast, and the world spreads a dinner for him, but no-one offers man supper but Jesus Christ. God only says 'At eventide it shall be light.' Christ only says, 'I will sup with him and he with Me.'"

A profane prodigal came to the service at Engedi, and while prayer was being offered, he, being in drink, began to rave and disturb. Perceiving his condition, the Revivalist addressed him sharply, bidding him to go out into the open air to get sober. The drunkard blenched at the rebuke and retreated; but before passing though the door he turned and said. "I am going, but remember that Moses the potman has a soul like yourself."

The audience and the preacher were staggered by this Parthian shot.

"Let us pray for him," said David Morgan. It seems that Moses halted also in the porch to listen to the prayer, and someone heard him say as he moved away, "O blessed prayer! Remember Moses the potman again!"

The Revivalist went to seek him on the morrow, and did not cease praying publicly for him until he received the welcome news that Moses had escaped from Satan's snare.

"Though he had lien among the pots, yet was he as the wings of a dove covered with silver, and her feathers with yellow gold."

This service resulted in 47 converts.

Moses built for himself a house of turf on Snowdon, where he prepared tea and coffee for visitors. One Sunday two strangers in drink broke the peace on the mountain, In the times of ignorance, Moses had been a champion fighter on the streets of Caernarfon, and though he had deserted the trade, he had not sold the tools, as the two Sabbath desecrators found to their sorrow, when he knocked their heads together, informing them at the same time, "You are under the law of Moses here."

During this visit, David Morgan offered a moving prayer on behalf of the sailors of Caernarfon, bereft of the privileges of the Revival owing to their profession. A Caernarfon boat, timber-laden, was making its way from Quebec at this time. One day Captain Elsby called all hands but two in the cabin for worship, which was usual; but on this occasion some extraordinary power fell upon them, resulting in rapture and rejoicing; and the Captain announced a "society", when every one remained to offer himself to God, a number of them never having done so before. When they made this known at Caernarfon, notes were compared, and the hour of the prayer on land was found to correspond with that of the "rapture" at sea.

A party from Caeathro were on the way to the Bangor Association, when the train stopped with a jerk in the tunnel near the city. Many were terror-stricken at finding themselves in total darkness, but one lady began to rejoice, saying "I am in a train that will never stop in the dark. 'He that believeth in the Son shall not come into condemnation, but is passed from death unto life." At this time the Revival had not touched Caeathro, but about a month later, a brother at the opening of a prayer meeting gave out with striking authority and light a few quaint lines to sing. Fourteen were convicted of sin in that service according to the augury of the initial hymn.

An able musician belonging to this church was sorely tired by the "confusion worse confounded" which the enthusiasm of an unmusical old brother wrought in one of the tunes of the sanctuary.

"You haven't got the right measure, Richard Jones," he protested.

"Never mind he metre, Humphrey bach." replied the old man, swaying to the rhythm of his own soul: "I am not singing by measure tonight, but by weight,"

The brotherhood at Capel Uchaf prepared for the Revival by enlarging the chapel. They proved their faith by building bigger barns for the anticipated harvest. When faith and works co-operate, the windows of Heaven will not remain shut. Perceiving the valley made of ditches, the Spirit of God descended like a flood from the eternal hills, replenishing them with fullness of blessing.

The mother of the Rev John Jones, Brynrodyn, was an old lady of remarkable spiritual characteristics. Apostrophising the saviour on a high hour of rapture, she cried, "O my beloved Child! We are afraid of Thy Father, but we love His Son!"

There was among the converts at Clynnog a young man of a handsome appearance, with a crop of curly golden hair.

"Are your parents alive?" asked David Morgan.

"No."

"Did they die in faith?"

"Yes."

"How many brothers and sisters have you?"

"Six."

"Are they Christians?"

"Yes."

Lifting up his voice, the Revivalist cried sweetly, "Here is the last in the Ark, let the deluge come when it will." Drawing his fingers through the lad's yellow ringlets, he added, "It would be a pity for the devil to get these. He always wants the young and the lovely. Thou art a beautiful lad – too beautiful for hell to get thee."

On this, the youth leaped on his feet, threw his arms around the neck of the Revivalist and kissed him. This scene threw the whole church into a delirium of rapture. David Morgan approached an old sister, who was like Miriam among the women.

"You then have cause to praise Jesus Christ, have you?"

"Thank Him for ever, I have," she replied.

"What has He given you? Has He ever given you a fine coach or a pair of horses?"

"No."

"Has He given you a palace?"

"What has He given you, then, that you praise Him like this?"

"To know Him, my boy," replied the old saint.

One evening a backslider returned to the fold at Y Felinheli (then known as Port Dinorwic). The ring of genuine penitence was absent from his testimony, so that he was not spared from being challenged. He was stung into self-defence and retorted curtly, "I am nothing worse than a sinner.

"Man!" thundered the old minister at him, "there is nothing worse than a sinner in the depths of hell!"

A milkseller was converted at Pwllheli, whose street cry had always been, "Cream! Cream!". It was observed that his call on the morrow of his conversion was "Milk! Milk!"

Nearly 400 new members were added to Penmount CM chapel in Pwllheli alone. A weekly class was established to read Dr Lewis Edwards's "Doctrine of the Atonement," and it was those converts who underwent the mental discipline of that class that developed into pillars of the church.

At Edern lived an eminent minister, the Rev Griffith Hughes, who wrote as follows in his diary: "I have experienced in this Revival much of the joy of religion, more than since 1832, and none of the troubles of that time. This is the third Revival within my memory; the others, 1819, when I joined the church, and 1832; but this is the greatest of the three."

When David Morgan preached at Edern, a large number were brought in. "I don't know how in the world I'll manage to shepherd them," said Griffith Hughes.

"It will be easier for you to shepherd them in the fold than on the common," retorted the Revivalist.

One of the deacons said later to Mr Hughes, "The Revivalist was very successful tonight, was he not?"

"Yes, he has a fair time of it," said the old pastor; "he only catches the fish, it is we that will have to salt them."

The subject of the Society at a Monthly Meeting at Fourcrosses (now called Y Ffor) during the Revival was Psalm 15. Thomas Williams, Rhyd-Ddu, was called upon for a five minutes' address. "'Who shall dwell in Thy holy hill?' - to dwell there is the great thing," said the old preacher. "I live on the slopes of Snowdon. Many visitors come there in summer, but we don't see a sight of any of them in the winter. There are many visitors to the Hill of Zion in the sunshine of the Revival, but to dwell there, summer and winter is the great thing."

When Captain Griffith "remained behind" at Llwyndyrus the old deacon told him, "We have long expected you; what made you stay tonight?"

"It was that verse which came to my mind, 'The water that I shall give him shall be in him a well of water springing up into everlasting life.'"

"What did you find in that?"

"I thought if I could but have that well within me, I'd never go on fire."

A servant lad at Brynmawr went out betimes on a wintry morning to cut gorse. A couple of hours later another of the men took the car to fetch what was cut. He found the gorse unchopped and the boy under the bushes on his knees. He touched him to recall him to his duty, and the contact seemed to magnetise him into the same state of rapt devotion as his friend. About mid-day the farmer grew anxious, and went to see what had happened; and he also was anointed with the oil of rejoicing. Neighbours gathered, and all who came found the gate of heaven on the gorse-heath.

The accounts from the Rev Thomas Phillips's book, published in 1860, capture the experiences of eyewitnesses in the various areas affected by the Revival. This touched the towns of Caernarfon,

Bangor, Pwllheli, Porthmadog, Tremadog Conwy and Llandudno to a blessed extent, but the the greatest advance of the gospel seemed in the slate quarrying areas, at Beddgelert, Waunfawr, Llanberis, Dinorwig, Pentir, Bethesda, Capel Curig, Betws-y-Coed, and Dolwyddelan.

The Rev Mr Griffiths of Bethel wrote as follows:

"The first place in which this wonderful religious movement developed itself in this part of the country is a populous neighbourhood about three or four miles eastward of Carnarvon, generally called Waunfawr. The people of God among the Independents and Calvinistic Methodists were eminently blessed with the 'spirit of grace and supplications'. Deep seriousness regarding Divine things seemed to pervade all minds. As a consequence many were turned to the Lord. Cases of the most marvellous conversions continually took place. In the course of a few weeks about 120 new members were added to the Calvinistic Methodists' Church in the neighbourhood, and upwards of 50 to that of our own. A few weeks ago the revival fire broke forth with marvellous power in the picturesque village of Cwmyglo, a place not far distant from the Dinorwic slate-quarries. Soon after this the whole surrounding country was in a blaze. Scenes resembling those which occurred on the Day of Pentecost were to be witnessed on every hand. Hundreds were pricked in their heart and cried out in deep agony, as of old, 'Men and brethren, what shall we do?' The Lord pours forth His Spirit with an abundance of grace far exceeding our highest expectations. The revival is manifesting itself among all religious denominations, but more especially among the Calvinistic Methodists and Independents, they being the most numerous and influential bodies in this part of the country. A spirit of unity and Christian love has been produced by the revival among the various sections of the Church of Christ, whose effects cannot but tell powerfully on the kingdom of darkness. A spirit of prayer has likewise possessed the Lord's people, which is really wonderful to behold. Our prayer-meetings have become exceedingly popular, and often there is an influence at work which cannot be gainsaid or withstood. The most contrite feelings are made manifest, while some of the most unlikely characters are melted down, and feel constrained to cry aloud for mercy. Our religious meetings now often continue until eleven or twelve o'clock at night, and scores of people retire from them to weep and to pray till the sun of another day dawns upon them. During the silent watches of the night the rocks of our country are to be heard resounding to the voice of prayer and praise, and our majestic mountains testify to the greatness of the work that is being carried out among us. A short time ago, a prayer-meeting for quarrymen was held on one of the mountains between Dinorwic and Bethesda slate-quarries. About four thousand persons attended, and the Lord graciously met His people. An eyewitness told me it was an occasion to be remembered while memory holds its seat.

"As yet, I am happy to state, there seems to be no abatement of the religious concern thus awakened in our country. It seems rather to advance and spread in all directions. Bethesda and the surrounding neighbourhoods, comprising a most populous and important district, have just caught the sacred flame of revival. A correspondent in the *Welsh Standard* or *Baner Cymru*, thus refers to the grand movement in this district:

"I rejoice in being able to inform your numerous readers that a most powerful revival has just broken out in Bethesda, and the various chapels adjacent thereto. On Saturday, September 3, prayer-meetings were held at two and six o'clock in the evening, and most remarkable meetings they were. God was truly among us. We have felt the Spirit of God at such meetings before; but nothing to what we experienced in these wonderful gatherings. After the meetings had passed away, loud praises were heard in the surrounding fields till midnight – one of the most wonderful things we ever witnessed. Besides the lateness of the hour, it rained heavily; still hundreds of people ran to the place whence issued this unwonted sound. It was found that several of those recently converted had retired to a field in the vicinity of Bethesda, and that, being overpowered by the spirit of God, they poured out their hearts joyfully before the throne of Divine grace. Some wept; others shouted, "Blessed be the name of God for thus remembering us in mercy." Others cried, "O Lord, save! Appear among us as a Saviour tomorrow; an infinite ransom has been found!" Others expressed thanks because God had saved them from the second death. Others, again, repeated some of the most exciting passages of Holy Writ, such as, "Oh that my head were waters, and mine eyes a fountain of tears, that I might weep day and night for the slain of the daughter of my people;" "Oh that they were wise, that they understood this, that they would consider their latter end." Before long, hundreds had assembled there, and the Spirit of God descended upon them in a wondrous manner, till all testified that God really was in that place. In the present movement we have been greatly struck by the fact that so much of the spirit of prayer has possessed the Lord's people. They draw the heaven of heavens, as it were, into every prayer-meeting; hence such congregations as were never before seen are brought together on these occasions. But, in every one of them, there is something more than a large congregation – the prayers penetrate the hearts of those who attend, whether they be male or female, even persons who never scarcely attended a place of worship are impressed; and the fact that people of this description are constrained to cry aloud, and fall down as if dead, proves beyond doubt that this movement is from God, and truly marvellous it is in our sight. I am happy to understand that revival is breaking out in other places, such as Carneddi, Llanllechid, and all the surrounding neighbourhoods.

"Three of the churches, under the joint pastoral care of my father and myself, have been signally blessed at this juncture. I have already alluded to the state of things at Waunfawr. The church at Bethel, again, has been wonderfully revived. Upwards of sixty new members have been added thereto in the course of a few weeks. At Shiloh, also, appearances are full of hope; more than twenty new members have been added to the church already."

The Rev W Ambrose, of Porthmadog, writes under the date of January 25: "We have had wonderful times here since I wrote to you last. I hope that hundreds have been really converted during the last two months. A large number of old, steady, respectable hearers have passed through a wonderful change. I have had the pleasure of seeing some, who were among my hearers when I came here, coming forward to make a profession of Christ after sitting twenty-three years under my ministry. The feeling of that moment I would not exchange for the feeling of an angel in heaven."

The Rev H G Edwards, incumbent of the new church at Llandinorwig, writes on February 13, 1860: "Several, I am happy to say, have been added to the church at this place, since the commencement of the revival. It began here in August last, and on the same Sunday night, in different places of worship in the neighbourhood. I do not believe the work has been more real anywhere than in this church, for it came upon us in a manner unsolicited, that is, without any effort on our part to create excitement. It came here like the wind, which 'bloweth where it listeth.' I shall never forget that Sunday night. There was nothing exciting in the subject of my discourse that evening, but the power which accompanied the word was very great, it was a melting power, a power which riveted the attention of every one present. I could see the furthest person in church, with his eyes fixed on the preacher. There was no noise, but, on the contrary, great stillness, and every one seemed to be listening for his life, and many were bathed in tears. In a few days after this, about sixteen joined the church at the same meeting. By this time the whole neighbourhood was in a blaze, prayer-meetings were held in the open air, as well as in places of worship, and scores were crying for mercy. The excitement has now subsided, but there is great life here still, and the new converts, with very few exceptions, have thus far remained faithful. There are many who ridicule the revival, but I can bear testimony to its good effects in these parts. The old members have been revived; many moral men, who had been 'halting between two opinions' for many years, have been able to 'decide for the Lord.' and some great sinners have been converted. As far as my own experience goes, I must say I should like to live and die in the blessed atmosphere of the revival."

From the Pennant slate quarries (Bethesda) we hear: "Strange and wonderful sights are witnessed here. The chapels are lighted up every night from seven to eight, nine, ten, eleven and twelve o'clock and sometimes until one and two in the morning. A great many persons, from the old man of fourscore to the child of five or six, have power with God and prevail, nor will they let Him go until they are blest. Truly, this is the greatest outpouring of His Spirit, as a Spirit of life and power, ever experienced by our nation and country. It is granted to all who use the key of fervent prayer, without any exception; but it would seem that the young people have the largest share, or, being their first love, they shew it more than others. In them the revival throws its effects far into the future. At one time our worldliness greatly hindered and injured our heavenly-mindedness; but now spiritual things absorb the attention, and nothing is heard but religious conversation in going and coming along the roads, in the works,in the shops, and other places. Ever since the Queen's visit, and the dreadful wreck of the Royal Charter, religion has been the great topic of the day."

Similar statements were made respecting the work at Pwllheli, Bangor, Carnarfon, Nefyn, and the whole of the districts called Lleyn and Eifionydd. Immense additions are made to the churches. In one month of the present year it is stated that one hundred and ninety one persons joined the communion of various denominations in the town of Pwllheli. In the letter communicating this intelligence it was said: "The meeting held at the Calvinistic Methodist on the night of January 20 was extraordinary. The sight was awfully stirring – young men who had been indifferent about their souls before, now cried out the loudest, 'What must we do to be saved?' while aged men with hoary hairs were as lively as lambs, praising God for visiting His people with showers of heavenly rain."

In the month of December last, a correspondent at Bangor states: "Although we have no loud expression of feeling under the ministry, we have among us warm hearts towards the Redeemer and His cause. In one day thirty persons joined the Calvinistic Methodists at the Tabernacle, and not a week passes without additions to all denominations in the city. There is a most powerful movement amongst the children. They meet to pray everywhere, in the roads, the houses, the school-rooms etc. They are full of the spirit of prayer, and it is remarkable what high and enlarged ideas they have, though expressed in humble language. They pray for all classes; sometimes a youth may be heard praying earnestly for an ungodly father, who was himself a month before a swearer and blasphemer. We know many examples of the kind. About twenty of these children have been admitted as candidates at Upper Bangor."

Later still, it is stated: "The good work continues to go on amongst the various congregations in the city and neighbourhood. Old hearers have been led to decide for Christ; backsliders are reclaimed; young people who had been religiously trained , but who had 'sold their birthright', are now seeking a home in the house of God; prodigals are returning to their offended Father, and many young children are under deep religious impressions.... We 'rejoice', but it is 'with trembling.'"

The chapter of Thomas Phillips's book on the results of the Revival says this of Llanddeiniolen, near Caernarfon, where the tidings are cheering: "I have before me the returns for six weeks only, viz, from September 1 to October 10. During this period, there were added to the Calvinistic Methodist churches in the parish, 368; to the Independents, 180; to the Wesleyans, 67; to the Baptists. 40; and to the Episcopal Church, 65 – making the total of fresh communicants, or candidates for communion, 720."

From Llanrug, near Caernarfon, came the following news: "More than 140 persons have been added to us in one month, and although the great excitement does not continue, I trust we shall go on increasing."

At and near Bethesda about 12 public houses were closed, partly on account of the change in the views of the parties who held them, and partly because the hope of profit from this business had quite disappeared.

A correspondent from the neighbourhood of Caernarfon says: "There is not only less drinking than usual, but fewer public houses – two have been closed at Ebenezer and Clwt-y-bont. A trial of the effects of the revival on the young men of the quarries was made in the last winter fair at Carnarvon. They generally took the lead in drunkenness and dissipation, but how different the scene last time! Instead of spending their time in the taverns drinking and feasting, they held meetings to pray for the salvation of sinners and to praise God for their own conversions. A prayer-meeting, long to be remembered, was held at Pendref chapel on the fair night, and another on the second day of the fair at Moriah chapel at two o'clock in the afternoon. The fair throughout was such as had never been seen before. The public houses were nearly empty, and all appeared to attend to their proper business. A landlord's daughter was asked, 'What kind of a fair have you had this year?"

The reply was "The people called for something to eat as usual, but there was very little drinking." On their return home, the young people testified how much more happy they were now when able to go and return from the fair, without following the usual practice of drinking to excess. It was only 12 months before, that many of them had been guilty of drinking, quarrelling, and fighting. Now, for the first time, they had found that the way of duty is the way of pleasure and safety.

The Rev Mr Griffith said the following about the awakening at Llanrug and Cwm-y-glo: "The drunkards, swearers and Sabbath-breakers are now seeking pardon from that merciful God whom they have offended, and are endeavouring to flee from the wrath to come. One hardened young man, who often got drunk, said to some of his companions that this wonderful work would not cause him to forsake his evil ways; but in less than half an hour he was seized with a feeling that caused him to cry out for mercy, or he would eternally perish. He is now amongst them a sinner saved through grace. Another young man said he would get something to drink, so as to be fit to persecute those of his acquaintances that he knew were assembled there. He approached the place and shouted, "I am Saul of Tarsus coming to persecute you, lads", but before he left the place, he became sober enough and began to cry for mercy, and was laid low at the foot of the cross.

The following report was written about Llanddeiniolen: "The good effects of the revival may be seen on the entire neighbourhood, as well as upon those who have made a formal profession of religion. There is a general change throughout the quarries. The cursing and swearing, with the light and profane conversations have ceased; we have prayer-meetings instead, and seriousness is stamped on every countenance. The most thoughtless are ready to acknowledge that something extraordinary has taken place, and one has said, that 'the days of earth are now like the days of heaven.' Not only is there less drinking, but the public-houses are decreasing in number; two have been closed lately at Ebenezer and Clwt-y-bont."

At Llanberis it was reported in October 1859: "From the commencement of the revival until the present time, we have had an addition of ninety persons, most of whom are young people who have spent their days in idleness, drunkenness and swearing, taking the Lord's name in vain – and were as unconcerned about religion and their souls as the brute beasts. Within the last few years, we found a generation of hardened young people springing up among us, totally devoid of the fear of God. But by this time, the young people are thoroughly humbled – easily entreated – kind and very liberal in their contributions towards the Redeemer's cause."

At Llanllechid there was this report: "Since the commencement of the revival among us, the neighbourhood presents a new aspect. It may be said that we have a 'new heaven' in the chapel and a 'new earth' in the roads and the fields. Instead of prowling about the neighbourhood at night, the young men now assemble in the various places of worship to pray. Instead of the oaths and obscene language formerly used in every direction, we now hear the voice of praise all round. Formerly the young people attended in crowds at the close of the day, but this year there was hardly anything worth calling a fair. Prayer-meetings were held in the chapel at two in the afternoon, and again at seven in the evening" (November 1859).

Penmachno: "We are glad to be able to state that the spirit of the present revival has made its appearance in a body of good works – such as brotherly love, alms to the poor, visiting the sick, prayer for those who are still unsaved, doing good to all - and thus shew that we are not angry with men, but with their sins." (October 1859)

Bangor and Bethesda: "Before this gracious visitation, the moral state of this neighbourhood was most deplorable. The young people, especially appeared to grow worse and worse, shaking off every religious restraint, becoming more callous and thoughtless, and acting as though they though that religion was a barrier to mental vigour and progress. The openly ungodly and drunken portion of the community appeared to have been left to themselves, and to commit sin with greater boldness and presumption. The Christian Church seemed too feeble to make direct efforts to withstand these increasing evils.

"But, through the goodness of God, the state of our neighbourhood is completely changed. Many of the young people who had sold their religious birthright, and had gone astray through the influence of sin and the world, are now arrested, and brought back again into the Church of Christ. Many prodigals have been reclaimed, and with humble contrition have sought and found their Father's house. Rioting and drunkenness are rapidly decreasing, the public houses are emptied, the noisy mirth usually proceeding from such places is no longer heard, the coarse oaths and profane expressions are abandoned and hated, the most presumptuous are now afraid of sinning openly – the sermons heard, and the advice received long since, are now remembered by very many, and seem to come with fresh power, so as to awaken the conscience, and to fill the soul with anxious concern. This takes place at midnight in bed, on the roads , or when busily engaged at their work in the midst of the rocks. Thus God is saving the souls of men from sin and wrath! Life had been breathed into the dry bones, and already there is 'an exceeding great army' of quickened souls in this populous place and the surrounding district.

"Party spirit and sectarian contentions have disappeared – the narrowness and prejudice with which Christians of various denominations regarded each other are fast dying away – and instead of these things, we have instances of love, liberality and brotherly kindness, reminding us of many of the blessed admonitions given by our Lord to His disciples in His sermon on the mount.

"The spirit of prayer has been given us in a greater degree than; this is felt more or less by all who are under the influence of this revival. The people delight in prayer, and hence we hear of prayer in all sorts of places, and at all hours. There are not many families in which an altar has not been erected, on which the morning and evening sacrifices are offered. The gift of prayer also is given in a marvellous degree: those who can hardly speak at all on other subjects are eloquent before the throne of grace. The old hymns are more appreciated than ever, and some of the anthems and tunes recently introduced are put aside for the present, in order to give place to such as can be used by the whole congregation.

"The Bible also is valued in these days by very many who took no delight in it heretofore: its pages are anointed by the tears of many Maries and Marthas; its simple verses are as 'the refiner's fire, and the fuller's soap,' purifying and cleansing the unbelieving and worldly heart. It may be said that the Bible-marks of a spiritual change may be found in large numbers of those who have been the subjects of the present awakening – namely, humility, meekness, patience, watchfulness, reverence, and godly fear." (November 1859)

Ysgoldy, Llanddeiniolen: "The public-houses are nearly emptied, and much beer has become useless. The influence of religion on the mind will enable every man to take care of himself. The two chapels are become too small to contain the hearers, and we must shortly enlarge our sanctuaries." (January 1860).

One correspondent near Bangor wrote: "In several of the chapels prayer-meetings are held at five o'clock in the morning, and again in the quarries during the dinner hour, besides the meeting for prayer held every night. It is as if the whole day and the whole week were one uninterrupted Sabbath. It would be almost impossible for men in the present state to enjoy more communion with God. The house of clay can hardly stand more. I know many young persons and others who have spent whole nights in prayer, in the out-houses, barns, and woods, even when the cold weather has set in. They seem to forget that they are in the flesh."

The effect of the 1859 revival on the number of criminal cases before the Courts in the whole of Wales was drastic. In the 12 months before the outbreak of the Revival, 1809 criminal cases came before the Courts. In the 12 months following the Revival the total number recorded was 1,228. The decrease was 50% in Caernarfonshire, which was exceeded by Cardiganshire with 58%, Anglesey with 57% and Denbighshire in 54%, which had all experienced even greater impacts from David Morgan's ministry.

Illustration 6: Rev David Morgan was
instrumental in the 1859 Revival in Wales

The Rev Thomas Philips of Hereford summed up his verdict on the 1859 revival (which though it was a very recent phenomenon, which started in Cardiganshire slightly over 12 months before, and rather more recently elsewhere, had already had very obvious results), that it had been a season of blessed awakening of the church. Under its influence, divisions were healed, old feuds made up, and the "devils" of discord, envy and strife were cast out. A higher standard of Christian experience was attained. Many aged disciples felt as though their youth was renewed by the glorious sights that they beheld, the heavenly music they heard and the inward joy they experienced. The revival even brought unity among the denominations. At one time it was thought a great matter of union and co-operation in the simple but holy work of circulating the Bible, without note or comment; and when ministers and people of different creeds met in one place and spoke on the same platform, on a subject about which there is hardly room for doubt, it was regarded as a great virtue, and a considerable stretch of Christian liberality. But in the 1859 revival there were united meetings for prayer, held in churches and chapels, where clergy and lay-members of the establishment, ministers and office-bearers of the various nonconformist bodies alternately engage in prayer. Where there had been much bigotry, bickering and unpleasant feeling between parties, which had been present for years, there was now only co-operation, love and zeal, all appearing anxious to rival each other other in their efforts to save the few who remain unconverted.

The following statements had been made in the columns of a Welsh newspaper, by one who had frequent and extensive opportunities of becoming acquainted with the facts of the revival in different parts of the principality:

"1. The additions to the churches amount to many thousands, far greater than has ever been known in Wales within the same period of time.

"2. I have gathered from inquiry that not one person in every fifty of those who have assumed a profession of religion within the last four or six months, has relapsed into the world.

"3. The people generally have been solemnised and brought to think of religious things. I asked an individual near Machynlleth whether the morals of the people had improved; he replied, 'Oh, dear, yes, entirely'; and then turned to his wife for confirmation of his statement. 'Yes.' she said, 'they are; every day is a Sunday now.'

"4. A missionary spirit has taken possession of the churches. There is no limit to their desire to save the whole world.

"5. The ministers and preachers are anointed with fresh zeal, and are animated with a new spirit. The churches and their office-bearers are filled with the ardour of their 'first love.'

"6. There is a great increase of brotherly love amongst professing Christians, and more cordial co-operation amongst the various denominations in their efforts to do good, and to oppose the common enemy.

"These are undoubted facts; and I am sure they have not been produced by Satan; nor could they be effected by man without aid from above." (Glan Alun, October 1859).

The fact that both sexes met in the revival meetings which were full of emotionalism did lead to some accusations of revivals leading to an increase in immorality, a claim which is refuted by the following letter which appeared in the North Wales Chronicle on May 18, 1861:

A VINDICATION OF THE LATE REVIVAL IN WALES. To the Editor of the North Wales Chronicle. Sir, - Having observed in several letters which lately appeared in your valuable paper, hints thrown out that the late revival in Wales has resulted in an increase of immorality, and having been painfully impressed with the fulsome insinuations of one particularly of your correspondents, who called himself "A Lover of the Church as inducive to Godliness", who stated that the fact has become so notorious that the vast increase of illegitimate children in consequence of the revival has occasioned the public to call them plant y diwygiad, I beg you will have the goodness to copy into the columns of your widely circulated paper, the following letter of the Rev D Edwards, Rector of Festiniog, which appeared in the Northampton Herald of the 4th inst as a refutation of the palpable falsehood, which some one from Merionethshire had also been circulating in England. The Welsh people, with few exceptions that are hostile to the said religious movement, will be glad to learn, by the publicity of the following letter, that, after a strict investigation of the charge, it is found, that instead of an increase of the immorality alleged to exist, there has lately been a considerable decrease; and may the blessing of Almighty God attend every effort now made to wipe off entirely this stigma, that has remained too long attached to our beloved country. I am, Sir, Yours faithfully, ALIQUIS. HOW HAS THE LATE REVIVAL IN WALES AFFECTED THR MORAL CONDITION OF THE PEOPLE? To the Editor of the Northampton Herald. Festiniog Rectory, April 30th. Sir, -When my attention was called last Friday to another letter in your paper on the above question, by One who has lived much in Merionethshire. "I expected as a matter of course, that he came to print this time fully prepared either to recant or substantiate all the extraordinary statements in his former letter; but to my great disappointment, I find that he has done neither the one nor the other, but merely reiterated his former bare and unfounded assertions, without any emendation whatever. In my letter to the Rev Prebendary Venn, of Hereford, which at that gentleman's request you kindly admitted to the columns of your valuable paper, I ventured to question the truth of all the contents of your correspondent's letter, which appeared to me so recklessly written that I verily believed they were either instantaneously, under a degree of irritation, after listening to Mr Venn's address on the Welsh Revival, which would be opposed to his feelings, or as the party is unknown to me – that they were the past-prandial effusions of a brain partially deranged. It was a strong conviction to that effect which induced me to mention in my last that I very much doubted whether he himself believed what he had written. The statements made by him are the following: 1. That the late Revival in Wales was "a wild and strange delusion," and that it has not benefited the Church. 2. That "even Dissenters themselves say no, we never wish to see another Revival." 3. That "an undoubted result of the Revival is an enormous increase in the number of illegitimate children." 4. That "he knows a hamlet in Merionethshire consisting of six families, five of which were connected with the late Revival; that in each of the five, as the result of the Revival, an illegitimate child was born, and that the only family free from that immorality was the one which had not joined the Revival movement." As regards the two first statements, I refer him again to my former letter, in which every impartial reader of your paper will find, I trust, satisfactory replies. A reference is therein made to an increase during the Revival in the number of communicants of some scores, in two churches in Carnarvonshire, where the Revival was most prominent in North Wales, viz, Carnarvon itself and Llandinorwic, which is a new church, built by the late Mr Assheton Smith, in the neighbourhood of his slate quarries; also four churches were named in Cardiganshire. (where Revival commenced, and where it was more general than in any other county in the Principality) where, during the Revival, many scores were added to the number of communicants, and in some of them even as many as 200 or 300. I pointed out to him, lastly, my own churches, where at the time of the Revival, the number of communicants were trebled , Mark how this correspondent deals with those facts in his letter: Mr Edwards refers us to the Vicar of Carnarvon, a clergyman in Cardiganshire, and to his own curates. This is just a specimen of the reckless manner in which this correspondent writes. I have not referred him to one of my curates. I named, together with my own, a few churches in North and South Wales, where very large additions were made to the number of communicants during the Revival. I might have added four times as many where similar additions were made; even in this county I could, in addition to my own churches, name Llanycil, Bala, Llanfor, St David's, Trawsfynydd, Penrhyndeudraeth, &c, &c, which all received large accessions of communicants during the Revival. I could name scores more in South Wales that were similarly blessed, but cui bono? As far as this correspondent is concerned I would never take the trouble of replying to his letter, but I write principally to give the public a correct information of these facts, and in vindication of the marvellous work of God in our Principality. This correspondent states that the Dissenters have, with their utmost endeavours, "attempted to get up another Revival"; but, as it were with the same breath he represents them as saying: "No, we never wish to see another Revival." However, in his last letter, he confesses that he cannot name a single congregation among all the various denominations who have said "But, Sir, what annoys and grieves me most of all is the awful exaggeration of immorality he wishes to attach to my fellow-countrymen, especially in this county and to the obloquy he attempts to cast upon the work of Divine Grace among us. He makes no hesitation in alleging that "am undoubted result" of the Revival in Wales is an enormous increase in the number of illegitimate children! jI am happy in being now able to meet this abominable charge with an "undoubted" proof to the contrary. The result of the Revival in Wales, as I shall now show you, has been a decrease in the number of illegitimate children. Allow me to make a passing remark here. You are aware, Sir, that such are now the facilities between the two peoples, that it is almost impossible that a traitor can belie us in the very heart of England without our knowledge, even in the mountainous districts of North Wales. When this monstrous charge first reached us, we were thunderstruck, but when the panic was over, and the steam once up,we did not rest till it was thoroughly sifted, and an estimate made of the comparative degree of the immorality alleged to exist. I shall begin by refutation of the charge at the place where the Revival commenced, and trace it in its progress from Cardiganshire to Anglesea. The following is an extract of a letter received from Thomas Lloyd Davies, of Bronwydd, Esq, magistrate for the counties of Cardigan and Carmarthen, dated 31st March, 1861: - "I have no hesitation in giving my opinion as a magistrate, that there is no perceptible increase of bastardy cases in the district in which I act; and I believe, on the contrary, that during the last two years there has been, on the whole, a dimunition of this evil. I believe there is a healthier tone of public feeling on the question of social evil." Another gentleman of high respectability, whose office brings him to close connexion with Wales, in his letter of last week, writes thus on the subject touching Cardiganshire: - "It is gratifying to find that the number of illegitimate children is decreasing in this county. I have had a rare opportunity this week, at Aberystwyth, to put a plain question to nearly all the ministers, and a considerable number of elders, belonging to the most numerous denomination of Christians in Cardiganshire. I told them my reason for making the inquiry. Not only did the ministers state there was a diminution but laymen also, some of whom held high offices in the various unions, positively declared that a great improvement was taking place in this respect." The following is an extract of a letter from John Foulkes, of Aberdovey,

Esq, magistrate for the counties of Merioneth and Montgomery, dated 27th of March, 1861. "I answer yours by first post just to say that I have, by this morning's mail written to several registrars and, as regards the Aberdovey district, the charge is false. Our petty sessions is in a better state as to this great sin." Let it be borne in mind that the Revival prevailed in North Wales in the years 1859 and 1860. Will your correspondent condescend to regard things things so vulgar as figures, as well as facts? The said Mr Foulkes gives the number of illegitimate children registered in the Dolgelley districts in the years 1858, '59 and '60 thus: - 1858,. the number was 27, 1859, 26,. and 1860, only 18. Is this an increase or a decrease in the County of Merioneth. Mr J B Jones, of Bala, states that in that union, containing a population of 6,736 the number of illegitimate children is as follows: 1853, 17,1859, 14, 1860, 15. Does the comparison here show an enormous increase or a decrease? Mr Samuel Vaughan, Clerk of the Guardians in the Festiniog Union, writs thus to me, dating his letter April, 1861: - I beg leave to forward for your information the following account of illegitimate children registered in my district, which includes fifteen parishes, six in Carnarvonshire, and nine in Merionethshire, comprising the whole of the extensive slate quarries at Festiniog. The number of the illegitimate children registered as such in

the year ending 31st March in 1858, was 44, 1859, 43, 1860, 62, 1861, 46. This shows how little the late revival had to do with it. "Most correct, extensive, and valuable information has also been received from Mr John Thomas, Clerk to the Guardians of the Carnarvonshire and Bangor Unions. I beg to notice that Mr Thomas holds other offices also, which afford peculiar facilities for acquiring correct information on the subject in question; and his statements, as regards that large and populous portion of North Wales, ought to satisfy any reasonable enquirer as to the direction where the truth lies. He

states that the number of illegitimate children registered as such in the year ending 31st March, 1858, was 69; 1859, 48; 1860, 72; 1861, 53. Next, as regards the district comprising the whole population engaged in the late Mr Assheton Smith's extensive slate quarries, he states that the number in 1858 was 19; 1859, 13; 1860, 23; 1861, 15. He then adds that the revival commenced there in June, 1859, and that an inquiry should then be made from March, 1860, up to the present time, embracing a comparison with the number the three years previously; and that from the two statements we find, that taking the whole of the illegitimacy of the Carnarvonshire parishes of that union, instead of an enormous increase, a considerable decrease is made manifest as compared with the previous year. Mr Thomas gives us next the statistics for the Carnarvonshire parishes of the Bangor Union for the three years ending in March 1st in each year. Bangor district, including Bangor and Llandegai, from 1st March in each year. Bangor district, including Bangor and Llandegai, from 1st March 1858, to 1st March, 1859, 26; 1859 to 1860, 22; 1860 to 1861, 19. Next he gives Llanllechid district, including Llanllechid, Aber and Llanfairfechan from 1st March, 1858, to 1859, 19; from 1859 to 1860, 15; from 1860 to 1861, 13. I ask your correspondent again, does this account give us an enormous increase or a decrease? It is really painful to my feelings, Sir, to be thus obliged to arraign him before the bar of public justice, and expose his fallacy, but it is his own fault; he had no business to make these reckless false statements. He may consider me severe, but it is the truth, and not your humble servant, that wounds his feelings. I will close this statement, containing the base charge I have refuted, with the sensible remark made on this subject by the above-mentioned Mr John Thomas in his letter to the Rev Thos Phillips, in which he says "The writer you refer to appears to me to have come to the conclusion he did, not so much from an investigation into facts, as by reasoning a priori from the almost certain consequence of the assemblage of a great number of the different sexes together late at night, but he did not include in his calculation that mysterious influence which, at the time of the Revival, seemed to pervade the minds of the worst of men, and deter them from the commission of their most relished iniquities. That dread of sinning which kept the confirmed drunkard from the public-house until all the business of the publican had almost ceased would, one would think, in some degree, prevent the perpetration of other sins besides drunkenness." A word again on the fourth statement, and then I have done for the present with the One who has lived much in Merionethshire. "What a paltry excuse he makes against naming the said notorious hamlet." Now, Sir, to meet that objection, and to obviate the supposed exposure, let him write a private anonymous letter, to me, describing the place, and I will pledge my word that I will not name the hamlet," but merely report in your paper whether what he states be true or false respecting it. Thereby the thing will not be more public than it is at present, nor will his name transpire. Should he object to this the readers of your paper, and especially the Merionethshire folks, will put down this fourth statement in the same category as the rest. One of my friends, who has undertaken to investigate this matter, writes thus: - "All who have seen the statement respecting the unfortunate hamlet say they do not believe it. Nothing short of testimony on the spot will satisfy. I do not say that such a thing is impossible, but on the face of it there is the greatest improbability." My letter is already too lengthened, but I beg to state in conclusion that though this anonymous correspondent, after thus blaspheming the work of the Holy Spirit, by terming it in its character a wild and strange delusion," and in its result immorality, may now screen himself behind a fictitious name from the knowledge of his fellow creatures, yet let him not forget that he is discovered and well-known to that to that Omniscient Being whose eyes run to and fro throughout the whole earth, " and before whose awful tribunal we shall all soon be summoned. I have no ill-will towards him. I pray that his blind eyes may be opened, that he may yet be brought to repentance and may the Lord grant unto him that he may find mercy of the

Lord in that day." Tendering my humble apology for occupying so large a space of your valuable paper, I remain, Sir, yours faithfully, D. Edwards.

Richard Owen, Llangristiolus

Richard Owen of Llangristiolus was to be the leader of a revival in the 1880s which touched North Wales, including Caernarfonshire. He was born in Llangristiolus, in Anglesey, in 1839, and responded to the revival preaching of David Morgan in that village in 1859, and was led to give himself to preaching. He was for some time a lay preacher in his native district, and after a short stay at Bala College, he was ordained in the ministry. He became pastor at Holloway, London and afterwards at Cana, Anglesey.

The revival with which he was associated, commonly referred to as Diwygiad Richard Owen, started in 1882, and continued until his death in 1887, and affected a significant area of Wales. This followed a time, which lasted from 1859 to 1882 when any revivals that took place had been insignificant and merely local.

In the time after the 1859 revival the country had become more materialistic in its thinking, with less attention given to spiritual matters. A new generation arose with different interests from preceding ones, with secular education taking precedence over spiritual education, and a departure from the old standards.

The first to recognise these dangers was Professor Thomas Charles Edwards. Through his powerful preaching and his emphasis on the essential truths of the Gospel, he did a lot to avert this threat. In 1874 the evangelists Moody and Sankey visited Liverpool, and although they did not visit Wales, many ministers from Wales went to Liverpool to hear them, and the evangelists had a great influence on them.

There were in Anglesey a number of enthusiastic ministers who were eager to evangelise the island: the Revs John Richard Hughes, Brynteg, James Donne and Thomas Jones, Dwyran, and their ministry brought much fruit. In 1876 Richard Owen was invited to join these brothers, and his work was blessed in certain parts of Anglesey, including Holyhead, Caersalem Chapel (Mynydd Bodafon) and Parc, Llandyfrydog.

In 1882-83 Richard Owen visited Llŷn and Eifionydd where his ministry received great approval, as he was greatly used in the revival that broke out there that year. Saving sinners was the major object of his ministry, and his success in this work. Many were saved through his evangelism, and many tried to analyse the secret of his success, but nobody succeeded in explaining the power of his ministry, apart from the preacher being completely in the Holy Spirit's power.

He was completely submitted to the Holy Spirit's authority, and stood before the audiences as a messenger sent from Heaven, and presented the truths of the gospel as if he had the authority of the Almighty's throne behind him. If there were any defects in his presentation, the tone of his voice or anything else, these were soon forgotten because of the divine presence about him, and the divine power that made his preaching irresistible. There is no way to understand the special nature of Richard Owen's revival without knowing something of the religious history of the Revivalist himself.

Richard Owen was a notable example of a man who had been dedicated from his mother's womb, and called through grace to preach Christ to men. He saw this as the major purpose of his life, and believed that this was the reason for his calling. He felt a powerful spiritual influence from as early as three years of age, and considered the first 10 years of his life to be the most wonderful, powerful and most sanctified part of his life, and that the rest of his life was a mere recapitulation of this early period. He had exceptionally godly parents, who prayed consistently for their children.

Richard Owen often acknowledged his debt to his parents' good example. He had been brought up with the family devotions which were kept consistently and often with considerable anointing. As a schoolboy he was noted for his unusual seriousness, which drew the attention of the whole neighbourhood. He considered his little Bible to be his greatest treasure, which he took with him to school, and took every opportunity to read it, at school or when running errands for his parents. He memorised many verses from an early age, and before long these started to speak to him. His greatest pleasure was to listen to the Gospel in the chapel, and was often touched by the ministry of the Word, when he was young, so that he desired to shout and rejoice.

He was accepted as a full church member at the age of 10, and subsequently considered this to be the beginning of a new chapter in his life, the eight years before he started preaching. He was chosen as a teacher at Cana Sunday school when he was still only a boy, and as a representative on the Sunday Schools meeting at the age of 17.

When he was 20, David Morgan, the Revivalist visited Anglesey as part of his tour during the 1859 Revival, and preached at Llangristiolus on a weekday evening. This was a particularly difficult and disappointing meeting from the point of view of the Revivalist and congregation alike. David Morgan asked if anybody had sacrificed a night's sleep in praying for the Holy Spirit, but nobody had, though one elderly Christian said he promised to do this. David Morgan asked if anybody else would join the old man in promising to do the same, and a pale-faced young man promised this. This young man was Richard Owen, and he kept to his promise.

Richard Owen was anxiously careful to keep the spirit of the ministry live in his soul, by being persistent and vigilant about his personal religion and spiritual experience. He was severe in his self-discipline to keep himself worthy for his calling. He waited daily for direct answers to his prayers about his ministry, and depended completely on God for the success of his ministry. He considered much prayer and serious meditation as appropriate means for keeping himself as a worthy vessel for his work, and aimed to be a workman approved by God, rightly dividing the Word. These characteristics explain one of the peculiarities of the Richard Owen Revival, that of the personal influence of the revivalist himself, which was not so obviously the case with the Evan Roberts revival of 1904-5.

Y PARCH RICHARD OWEN,

(Y DIWYGIWR ENWOG.)

Illustration 7: The Rev Richard Owen, who was a major revivalist in the 1880s

Many people experienced things unknown to the world through the prayers and singing during the 1905 revival, even when the revivalist was absent from the meeting, but in the case of Richard Owen, the revivalist himself had a great influence on the meetings, especially through his exceptional seriousness and holy gaze. Even unbelievers felt in his presence the conviction that he was a vessel of honour, sanctified and prepared for every good work, and that they were listening to one of the holy men of God speaking to them as led by the Holy Spirit.

The Richard Owen revival has to be recognised, on account of its effects as a powerful move of God. If getting men to see themselves as sinners, to repent of their sins and turn to Christ as their only Saviour, and aim to live the rest of their lives for His glory are the powerful signs of the work of the Holy Spirit in the ministry of the Gospel , then thousands of examples of this could be seen in North Wales during the years 1884-5. People of all ages and all classes came to listen to Richard Owen, and it was rare that nobody was deeply touched by the truth that came from his lips. Men who had been listening for years, without feeling any conviction under the sound of the Gospel, or any influence from it, could be seen weeping, praying, praising God, and promising to live a changed life from then on.

From his success as a revivalist, one would imagine Richard Owen to be a particularly powerful preacher, but the following report relating to a meeting in Mold in 1884 shows that his power was not from any particular eloquence:

The religious revival services commenced here on Friday last, and those who anticipated a religious heat have not been disappointed. The Rev Richard Owen is not an eloquent, fiery preacher – quite the reverse, for he is simple, earnest and impressive, both in his manner and delivery, and, above all, is one who believes thoroughly in the power of prayer. Up to the time of writing, the services have been literally crammed, and the results so far are most satisfactory. (North Wales Express, March 14, 1884)

He eventually moved to Penygarnedd, Anglesey, where he died in 1887 at the age of 48, of an attack of asthma, after having preached at Pentraeth the previous Wednesday. He was one of the most popular preachers of his day, and during the last few years of his life, immense crowds flocked to hear him wherever he went. He was well-known in Rhyl and neighbourhood. He preached there many times, to enormous congregations, people coming from Rhuddlan, St Asaph, and all the places around to hear him. At Rhuddlan he carried on a very successful revival mission, and every night for about a week a score of people walked from Rhyl to attend the services. He had neither eloquence nor liveliness of gesture, and yet when he stood face to face with his congregation, and the inspiration of the moment was upon him, the lucidity of his thoughts and the vividness of his descriptions had an overwhelming effect.

When he died in 1887, it was claimed in the Caernarfon and Denbigh Herald that he could reckon no fewer than 13,000 converts through his ministry.

Although Richard Owen was the pre-eminent revivalist of the 1882-84 Revival, he was supported by a Caernarfonshire Wesleyan minister called Hugh Hughes (just as he had been supported, earlier in the 1870s by fellow Calvinistic Methodist John Richard Hughes).

The parallels with the 1859 Revival is striking, since at that time the Calvinistic Methodist Revivalist Humphrey Jones invited the Wesleyan David Morgan to join forces with him early on in that powerful move, so that they could work together to impact the nation. It is quite possible that Richard Owen took his cue from Humphrey Jones's example. Both of them were prepared the advance of the kingdom over loyalty to a denomination.

Hugh Hughes (1842-1933) was born in the Braich-talog district of Tregarth, just north of Bethesda, in the slate quarrying district, the son of Humphrey Hughes, a quarryman and his wife Jane. He was converted under the ministry of John Evans, Eglwysbach, and went on to minister mostly in North West Wales, beginning in 1866. However, he spent brief periods ministering among the Welsh communities of Liverpool and London. He was, for example, living in Tranmere, Birkenhead, at the time of the 1881 census. On one occasion, the railway company ran special trails to his meetings in Caernarfonshire, and over 500 were converted. During the revival of 1882-4, he was based in Llangollen, though by 1887 he had moved to Abergele. His wife Margaret Ellen Hughes, who had been born at Amlwch in 1845, died in Abergele in in 1902 aged 57. Hugh Hughes would outlive her by more than 30 years.

1904-5 Revival

Towards the end of the 19th century the authority of the church had been eroded by church leaders taking a more psychological and philosophical approach to Christianity. It can be said that the undermining of Christianity had ironically started in the very year of the 1859 Revival, through the appearance of Charles Darwin's book *On The Origin Of Species*, which offered an explanation of origins which did not require a Creator. The effects of this new explanation on the leadership would also impact on the congregation.

In the late 19th century the churches were very active from a social, cultural and educational viewpoint, but spiritually asleep. Teaching from the creeds and confessions of faith meant that Nonconformists and Anglicans alike knew had a good understanding of doctrine.

People were able to discuss doctrines such as assurance and the Holy Spirit from an intellectual level, but showed little desire for these to touch them spiritually.

Before any revival, whether in Wales or elsewhere, without exception there would be a period of time (sometimes years) in which people have prayed earnestly for God to send the fires of the Holy Spirit. Although there was much dryness in the church, there were many of the faithful who understood that Heaven had definite conditions before a true revival could be expected, and that the Church needed to be aware of its need for revival, and of its inability to go forward without the Lord's leading. Yet despite the labours of the Sunday school teachers and preachers in communicating the truths of the scriptures, and in warning, it seemed that their work was in vain, as the age seemed to be becoming more lukewarm and given to vanity and excess. It became clear to many that something greater than all of man's efforts was needed, and that is indeed what dawned when God visited His people.

The 1904-5 Revival in Wales was also to be influential in the development of the Pentecostal Movement which developed in California in the early 20th century, especially after the Azusa Street Revival of 1906-1908 in Los Angeles. The Pentecostals and the 1905 Welsh Revival both share an emphasis on music and on supernatural phenomena, which was taken to be the fulfilment of the Biblical prophecy of Joel chapter 2 of God pouring His spirit on all flesh, so that dreams and visions would become common. The 1905 Revival was also the occasion of the origins of the Apostolic Church in South Wales, which like the Pentecostals, practise the gift of tongues.

This Awakening also swept North America, Scandinavia, and the mission fields of India, Africa and Latin America.

The 1904-5 Revival came as the result of Evan Roberts being challenged by the Holy Spirit so that he felt that he had to leave the Bible College course he had just started, so that he could hold revival meetings. This particular move of the Holy Spirit was characterised by the large congregations seeming to have a mysterious instinct for knowing when to switch from prayer to praise, or to stop singing, and start praying instead. Very often there was no actual preaching, but Evan would illustrate doctrines by talking about things familiar from everyday experience.

The fact that generally the problem was not a lack of doctrinal knowledge, but a slowness to commit to the call of the Gospel, meant that this approach was in fact not an inappropriate one.

His informal, unconventional approach had caused a lot of controversy, and there were times he would rebuke members of the congregations for having come out of curiosity, and stopped having guest soloists when he detected a spirit of envy and competition coming in. There were even times when he would not turn up at a meeting because he claimed that the Holy Spirit had told him not to go.

He insisted that the Holy Spirit should be the only controller of the meetings. Such behaviour would be puzzling to outsiders, and inevitably there would be criticisms, not least from the Rev Peter Price, minister of Bethania, Dowlais, Merthyr Tydfil, who wrote a letter to the Western Mail in January of 1905, condemning the "so called revival".

The Rev Price was disturbed by what he considered to be the emotionalism and excesses of Evan Roberts's meetings, and argued that there were in fact two revivals running in parallel, namely a genuine work, and a bogus one which owned Evan Roberts as its originator.

An article in the Weekly Mail on February 4 condemns the Rev Peter Price's letter which it described as an "unjustifiable attack" which made serious assertions relating to the revivalist's sincerity. The Weekly Mail, while admitting that there may be a difference of opinion as to the revivalist's methods, and that his manner is open to criticism, nevertheless concluded as follows:

It is only fair that this Revival should be judged by the rule which is the criterion of all similar movements – its results. The Revival has been in progress now for about three months, and during that time has been the means of bringing some seventy thousand men and women to a sense of sin and duty. The bulk of these, so far, show no signs of wavering or backsliding, and the new and changed life they lead is known to their neighbours and friends. In fact, social life in Glamorgan and Monmouthshire has been transformed by this Revival. Its good fruits are met with everywhere.

The revival was already showing good fruit in its early stages, while it was still confined to South Wales. Inevitably people elsewhere, including Caernarfonshire, would read in the newspapers about what was happening in South Wales, and long to see the same things happening in their meetings, and it was not too long before this wish was granted.

The revival was already under way in Llanfairfechan before 1905, and a preaching meeting during the evening of November 28, 1904 at Caersalem Chapel seems to have been the beginning of a powerful revival in that quarrying village, with meetings later being held in Ysgol y Nant and Libanus Chapel. Following on from these services the quarrymen held prayer and praise meetings during their lunch hours at the brake hut.

It can be said that the quarrymen of Caernarfonshire were not idle in waiting for the revival, since in January 1905 at a missionary meeting in Skewen, South Wales, a North Wales minister was present, who reported that Snowdon was being shaken by the prayers of the quarrymen.

The following report from the Welsh Coast Pioneer and Review for North Cambria of March 3, 1905 makes it clear that the Revival was already having an impact in North Wales even before Evan Roberts arrived there:

South Carnarvonshire: The revival led to the abandonment of many of the annual St David's Day entertainments in South Carnarvonshire, including the Portmadoc Church Eisteddfod. Leek favours were much in evidence in Portmadoc, Pwllheli and Criccieth. The only meetings on Portmadoc were big revival services conducted by the Rev Penar Griffith, of Swansea, at the Memorial Congregational Chapel. A special service for women in the afternoon was attended by as many as 800. A tea and concert were given at Criccieth. The Young Men's Association of Pwllheli held a dinner at the Eifl Hotel on St David's Eve, and on Thursday the Conservative Club held their annual banquet at the Crown Hotel.

Evan Roberts reached North Wales in April 1905, after his mission in Liverpool. He arrived in Capel Curig on April 18, where he rested for a few days before his mission in Anglesey, which took place from May 16 to July 3, and attended the singing festival in Bethesda on Sunday, April 21, and visited many places of interest, including Beddgelert, the cradle of the mighty revival of 1817-22, before going to Cemaes, Anglesey on May 16.

The following report from the Llandudno Advertiser of May 13, 1905, describes his visit to Beddgelert:

MR EVAN ROBERTS AND HIS WAY WITH WELSH CHILDREN: Mr Evan Roberts on Tuesday visited Beddgelert, the "capital" of Snowdonia, driving thither in company of the Revs John Williams, G Ellis (Bootle). Dr M Affie, and H H Soberts (Capelbury). While at tea at the Prince Llewelyn Hotel a message came from the Vicar (the Rev J Jenkins) stating that the children of the village were being treated to tea, and inquiring whether Mr Roberts would say a few words to them in a field close by, where they were indulging in games. Mr Roberts immediately consented, and after a short speech on the need of doing everything thoroughly got each child to say "I will do my best". The Calvinistic Methodist Chapel which stood close by. It had in the meantime been opened, and the villagers flocked into the building in large numbers, in the hope that the revivalist would hold a short service. Many women rushed in bare-headed and with their aprons on. Their hopes were realised, and in the course of a short service, Mr Roberts delivered an address on "God is love". Before leaving Beddgelert the party visited the famous Aberglaslyn Pass. Mr Roberts made an entry in the visitors book at the hotel, alluding to the great revival in Beddgelert early in the last century."

The mission in North Wales mostly concentrated on Anglesey, with a few visits in Caernarfonshire, but the more conservative nature of the people of North Wales meant that the mission took on a different character from the meetings in South Wales. The people of North Wales preferred a more traditional form of preaching, while the local ministers also exercised more control. As a result there were fewer incidences of spontaneous singing, groaning and impromptu prayers than occurred in the South, and as a result the services were generally more conventional in their nature.

His itinerary, organised by his friend, Dr John Williams, mostly covered Anglesey, but included an anniversary at Abererch, near Pwllheli, on June 3, and when people heard of his arrival the chapel was soon filled. On the Sunday evening, June 4, the village's chapels could not hold all the people, so a stage had to be set up in a farm yard.

After his mission in Anglesey which lasted a month he was asked to hold two meetings on July 4 at the Pavilion in Caernarfon, which was capable of seating 10,000 people. The first meeting was announced to start at 2pm, but the huge venue was full long before that time, Excursions ran in from all the surrounding country, and the streets were thronged at noon. This was an united meeting for Anglesey and Caernarfonshire, organised by the local Free Church Council.

Before Evan Roberts arrived, the meeting had been in progress, full of spontaneity, but without intense fervour. The Revivalist preached, and every word could be heard in all parts of the building and his words created great enthusiasm.

In a sense there were actually two meetings, but since there was only an hour interval between them, in effect it was one huge meeting which started at 11.30am and finished at 8pm. Hundreds remained in the Pavilion for the evening meeting, fearing that there would be no room for them if they left. The throng increased greatly for the evening service, and although 12,000 entered the building, many had to return.

The enthusiasm of this evening meeting was much greater than that at the afternoon one.

It was at massive meetings like the one at Caernarfon's National Eisteddfod Pavilion that Evan Roberts tended to speak most severely, as he was aware that he was surrounded by church leaders and staid chapelgoers, who needed the vision to pray for the lost, and the courage to witness to them. Even those who had just been saved, were more interested in the spectacular aspects of the revival, and showed insufficient concern for the lost.

His four points about witnessing were (1) Confess Christ, not just as an initial act of salvation, but as a constant witnessing, (2) Put away any doubtful thing, thus avoiding anything that could hinder one's witness. (3) Obey the Spirit. (4) Witness in every possible form.

After his meetings in Caernarfon he went to Bala before returning to Glamorganshire for a time.

He rested most of the time after the Anglesey and Caernarfon mission, and returned to Caernarfonshire from December 6 to January 14, 1906, at the invitation of the Caernarfonshire Free Churches Council. This mission followed the pattern of his previous ones. There was no order of service. Everyone was left free to speak when the Spirit prompted him. In all the meetings there was no lack of spontaneity. Some of them were equal in fervour to many of the most intense ones of the previous journeys. The mission stirred the churches considerably, and was the means of adding many to their number. It is supposed that his meetings with the young people and the children were about the most successful of anything in his history. Like the Anglesey mission of summer 1905 it left a lasting effect on Caernarfonshire.

One difference is that this time he did not take anyone with him, not even his sister. He believed that he was divinely directed to go alone. A seven weeks' mission was arranged, answering to the seven districts into which the county was arranged. It was to commence at Pwllheli on December 4, and end at Llanberis on January 18. A whole week was to be given to each district, conducting meetings nightly. The general committee decided to relieve him on Sundays, owing to the strain the work entailed. The campaign started at Pwllheli on December 4, according to the original arrangement. But soon appeals came urging the Missioner to conduct two meetings daily in order to avoid overcrowding at certain centres. He did this on several instances.

On December 21, 1906, Y Cymro reported that he had successful meetings in Llithfaen, Penygroes, Talsarn, Llanllyfni and Brynaerau. Although he preached very effectively, there were not many converts, but this could be attributed to the fact that almost all the audiences were already church members.

He went out to country places during the day, thinking that people would not follow him during the nights, but after him they went. Before the journey was finished, a General Election had been called. Evan Roberts and the committee did not feel that the excitement of an election was consistent with the spirit of the Revival meetings, and therefore the journey came to an end at Brynrodyn on January 14.

In February, 1906, it was announced that the mission was to recommence in Bangor the following month, after the election.

The Evening express of February 9, 1906 reported that the secretary of the Bangor Free Church Council had received a letter from Evan Roberts, in response to her letter asking when he proposed to resume the North Wales mission. He replied that he was unable to give a specific date or make any arrangements because he had "no light" on the subject. The newspaper then reported that "The inference is drawn from this letter that the mission is abandoned, if not permanently, at least till next autumn." As it transpired, the inference was justified.

However, the Weekly Mail of April 18, 1906 reported that the mission was not about to resume:
NO MESSAGE FOR BANGOR. MR EVAN ROBERTS REFUSES TO HOLD A MISSION. Mr Evan Roberts, who has been attending the meetings of the Keswick Convention at Bangor this week, has been pressed to remain over next week and conduct a series of meetings on his own account. He replied to the effect that he did not feel that he had any message from God for Bangor, and did not really know when he would be called to come to Bangor.

His attendance at the Keswick Convention was not as a speaker, but as a private individual, and sat unobtrusively in one of the pews .The Weekly Mail of April 21 reported that there was not a large attendance of the general public before it became known he was there, and he was followed by women and children as he tried to make his way back to his lodgings.

The pressure of the mission, and the fact that the revivalist was thronged by crowds wherever he went, including conventions which he attended as a private individual, would have been daunting, so it might not be surprising that he was to fall into a deep depression in the spring of 1906, and was invited to convalesce at the home of Jessie Penn-Lewis in Leicestershire, and that the projected resumption of the North Wales mission did not take place .

Illustration 8: Evan Roberts's last meeting of his tour in Anglesey, at Llanfair PG. This scene would have been quite a familiar one, as so many of his meetings were held in open fields

As can reasonably be expected the revival was not good news for pubs, as sobriety became more prevalent, but was very beneficial for the sale of Bibles, as shops sold their entire stocks of Bibles.

While some people attribute his failure to get people to be concerned for the lost to his failure to provide a foundation of exposition and instruction, there is little evidence that the ministries of the Revs WS Jones and RB Jones in North Wales had any deeper and more lasting effects.

Is another revival likely?

In the past revivals were relatively regular events, so that the previous revival was a fairly fresh memory, but the most recent widespread revival was in 1904-5, over a century ago.

In the 19th century authoritative preaching was much more common than today, and an acceptance of the supernatural side of Christianity was more prevalent, while today a more "scientific" viewpoint seems to be dominant, with evolution being widely accepted as an explanation of creation. In some ways it would seem that the 19th century was a more favourable time for revivals.

However, we need to remember that the spiritual state of Anglesey (and the United Kingdom in general) in the 1730s was just as bleak as today, and yet the Methodist Revival and the Great Awakening started at precisely that time.

Knowing that God could and has done mighty works in the past gives a strong encouragement to plead with Him to do a similar work again, and as in the past, it is precisely when the Church humbles itself in prayer that He will start working.

Further reading

Bennett, Peter and Dorothy: The Quarry Revival, Turning Point, Llanfairfechan.

Dodd, AH: A History of Caernarfonshire, Bridge Books, Wrexham (1990)

Davies, Eryl: The Beddgelert Revival, Evangelical Press, Bridgend (2004).

Evans, Eifion: Revival Comes to Wales, Evangelical Press, Bridgend (1967)

Jones, Brynmor Pierce: An Instrument of Revival: Complete Life of Evan Roberts 1878-1951)

Morgan, J J: The 59 Revival in Wales, |J J Morgan, Mold (1909)

Owen, Hugh: Hanes MC Mon, Liverpool (1937).

Philips, Rev DM: Evan Roberts, the Great Welsh Revivalist and his work, Quinta Press, Weston Rhyn (2004).

Philips, Rev Thomas: The Welsh Revival: Its Origin and Development, James Nisbet and Co, London, (1860)

Pritchard, John: Methodistiaeth Môn, D Jones, Amlwch (1888)

Useful websites

https://daibach-welldigger.blogspot.com/[1] This blog seeks to honour the work of the Holy Spirit in Wales through accounts of people, places and events. As can be expected, there is a wealth of information on all aspects of Christianity in Wales.

http://www.ukwells.org/ This site touches on the sites and prominent figures connected to revivals and awakenings all over the United Kingdom, and is an invaluable tool for in-depth study.

www.revival-library.org/[2] Largest collection of digitised Revival and Pentecostal texts on the World Wide Web!

Page

---

1. https://daibach-welldigger.blogspot.com/

2.   http://www.revival-library.org/

Also by Iolo Griffiths

About the Author

Iolo Griffiths was brought up in Anglesey, lives in North Wales and has been working for Trinity Mirror North Wales since 1987, firstly as a librarian and then proofreader, and then a journalist. He is now a Community Content Curator for Trinity Mirror North Wales His main interests are genealogy and local history (mainly North West Wales)

Read more at https://www.facebook.com/IoloGriffithsAuthor/.

Ingram Content Group UK Ltd.
Milton Keynes UK
UKHW031807080523
421401UK00009B/746